CONTROLLING THE

ARMS TRADE

THE WEST versus

THE REST

PAUL CORNISH

Bowerdean Briefings
SERIES EDITOR: PETER COLLINS

BOWERDEAN
Publishing Company Limited

First published in 1996 by the Bowerdean Publishing Company Ltd.
of 8 Abbotstone Road, London SW15 1QR

British Library Cataloguing-in-Publication Data:
A catalogue record for this book is available from the British Library.

ISBN 0 906097 44 4

Designed by the Senate.

Printed in Malta by Interprint Limited

CONTENTS

GLOSSARY AND ABBREVIATIONS

ACDA	(US) Arms Control and Disarmament Agency
AG	Australia Group
CFE	Conventional Forces in Europe Treaty
CoCom	Co-ordinating Committee for Multilateral Export Controls
CRS	(US) Congressional Research Service
CSCE	Conference on Security and Co-operation in Europe
G7	Group of Seven Industrialized Nations
MTCR	Missile Technology Control Regime
NATO	North Atlantic Treaty Organization
OPEC	Organization of Petroleum Exporting Countries
OSCE	Organization for Security and Co-operation in Europe
P5	Permanent Five (members of the UN Security Council)
SIPRI	Stockholm International Peace Research Institute
UN	United Nations
UNDC	United Nations Disarmament Committee
WMD	Weapons of Mass Destruction

I

INTRODUCTION

This book examines key aspects of the international arms trade as it has developed since the end of the Cold War. The relaxation of East–West tension had a dramatic effect on the international market for weapons and military equipment, and the technology needed to build and use them. The end of the Cold War also led to a series of initiatives, by the United Nations and by groups of governments, to control, or at least to supervise, the market. The book is primarily concerned with the trade in 'conventional' weapons and weapons platforms, such as armoured fighting vehicles, artillery and mortar systems, combat aircraft and warships, and associated technology. Weapons which do not come under the 'conventional' category include nuclear, biological and chemical weapons of mass destruction (WMD), although mention will be made of some of the problems and lessons of WMD non-proliferation initiatives. The book also focuses mainly on official, government-to-government arms and technology transfers, and addresses only briefly the illegal or covert international trade in military equipment.

As the Cold War drew to a close from the mid-1980s, military spending around the world began to fall. Domestic arms markets contracted and the size of the global trade in weapons, military equipment and related technology began a steep decline. But the international arms market not only shrank; its character and dynamics – along with the whole field of defence manufacturing – also began to change dramatically. With mounting public pressure for a 'peace dividend', and the acceptance by most governments that Cold War levels of military spending and deployment were no longer necessary or justifiable, the Cold War protagonists soon found themselves with large excesses in defence manufacturing capacity. In response, defence industries and governments identified a number of possible courses of action, including *conversion* to non-military production, *diversification* out of defence manufacturing altogether, industrial *consolidation and restructuring* within the defence sector, and *weapons exports*.

Conversion of manufacturing plants from military to civilian production (e.g., making television sets in a defence electronics factory) was widely discussed but was soon perceived to be something less than the cure-all for which many had hoped. In the West, the claims for defence conversion were met with a sceptical response, particularly from those governments which took a free-market, non-interventionist approach to defence industrial restructuring after the Cold War, and which argued that the healthiest way to adjust to changed circumstances was to allow the market to take its course (and its toll). In the former Soviet Union and its allies, it was realized that the only marketable, hard currency-earning commodity was weapons – good, relatively cheap 'swords', rather than badly marketed, over-engineered 'ploughshares' – and an elaborate and ambitious defence conversion programme met with little success. Structured (i.e., government-organized), rather than market-led, defence conversion does, nevertheless, continue to be discussed as a possible option. Diversification, whereby defence industries, conglomerates and multi-nationals would expand and acquire non-military sectors, met with a more favourable response in industry, especially in the West. But diversification proved to be difficult, and many firms found that expertise and knowledge accumulated in the defence sector did not travel well. The third option was received rather more favourably. To date, a great deal of effort has been devoted to national and international restructuring and consolidation in the defence sector. In spite of ostensibly adverse market conditions, some firms have even shaken off their non-military interests altogether and concentrated still more closely on the defence sector.

With narrowing prospects for overseas sales making it appear at best an ambitious goal, the fourth option – expanding export sales – was nevertheless also seized upon by defence industry. At a time of global recession, governments, too, were interested in a course which could enable 'vital' or 'strategic' national industries to be sustained, unit production costs to be reduced and further research and development to be funded. The scene was thus set for what one analyst of the international arms market has called a 'new age of export driven proliferation' (Willett, p.114). With similar conclusions being reached throughout the defence manufacturing world, the result is that the supposedly more peaceful, less antagonistic post-Cold War world has an arms market which, although considerably smaller, is in many respects more diverse, vigorous and competitive than its Cold War predecessor. With huge excesses in supply combined with declining demand, it is also a market in which much of the initiative has shifted to the buyer. As this shift has taken place, so the struggle for market share has become increasingly energetic. Defence export decisions are becoming ever more responsive to commercial considerations and contracts are becoming increasingly complex, often involving the transfer of manufacturing plants, 'know-how' and key, sensitive technologies through off-set and counter-trade arrangements.

The development of the buyer's market also inhibits efforts to control defence related trade. At the national level, no matter how rigorous their export control policies and practices, individual governments see that the glut of old and new suppliers means that any decision to deny a given export might simply result in the buyer going elsewhere; the complaint (or excuse) that 'if we don't export, others will' has been heard increasingly in recent years. Competition for market share also diminishes the chance for wider supply-side consensus on the control of exports of certain weapons or technologies to certain destinations, making multilateral supply-side regulation of defence trade increasingly difficult.

The end of the Cold War not only saw the advantage, in market terms, passing to the buyer, it also saw the buyer becoming rather more self-assured. During the Cold War, Non-Aligned or Third World states perceived themselves to be in a struggle to achieve the dignity and respect due to them as full members of the international system of states. Nowhere was the sense of dissatisfaction more plain than in the United Nations. As its membership expanded rapidly during the 1950s and 1960s, so discrepancies were perceived between the United Nations' Charter's promises regarding the sovereign equality of states, and the *realpolitik* of a world dominated by the superpower confrontation. But with the passing of the Cold War, it is as if the high-minded promises made in the UN Charter are now expected to be honoured. Aware of their increasing importance in the international economic system, Third World states have become far less willing to accept second class status. For these states, the end of the Cold War amounts to the triumph of nationhood and state sovereignty, and the end of the decades-long struggle for decolonization and full membership of the international system. Their sense of frustration has been apparent for many years, but what distinguishes the current mood is that many governments and leaders now feel able to add substance to the rhetoric. Technological, economic and even military advantages are still enjoyed by the West/North, and there is no doubt that these advantages confer a certain authority and bargaining strength over Third World customers. But as these states assume an increasingly important role in the global economy, the West's capacity to 'leverage' or merely influence the Third World is likely to become more limited.

With manufacturers anxious to sell, particularly in the expanding market of the Asia–Pacific region and elsewhere, and with an increasingly assertive and self-confident clientele, the international trade in conventional weapons and related technology is altering in two important ways. First, with so much more now being heard of a state's long-established right, under Article 51 of the UN Charter, to defend itself and, by extension, to decide for itself what, and from whom, to buy in the arms market, the manufacture of weapons and the trade in them are increasingly seen in national terms. The ownership of modern conventional weapons, and the ability to manufacture them, are now widely held to be normal, inalienable and even essential attributes of a modern, sovereign nation-state. What is becoming increasingly clear is that an important dynamic behind the modern arms trade – and a major obstacle to its regulation – is this new, self-confident nationalism of the post-Cold War era.

The second important feature of the post-Cold War arms trade is the absence of an internationally accepted, central organizing principle or set of standards upon which to build some form of control regime. Many of the conditions which underpinned the hegemonic arms trade relationships of the Cold War have now been undermined. It is no longer possible to describe the international arms trade primarily as an extension of East–West power politics, nor even as the manifestation of the foreign policy of the world's weapon manufacturers and suppliers. But if it is clear that the international arms trade is no longer organized along the relatively simple lines of Cold War power politics, it is much less obvious what, if anything, could provide a new organizational core. The international arms market is more commercially oriented than at any time during the Cold War, but it seems unlikely that market forces alone will be able to provide the political and moral principles and procedures in accordance with which the trade should, arguably, be regulated. With the 'new world order' offering very little in the way of controlling mechanisms, even at the most basic level of Cold War-style spheres of influence, something approaching political and economic free trade in arms may have arrived.

In August 1990 Iraq invaded Kuwait and the ostensibly revitalized United Nations and the 'international community' faced their first major challenge. Following Iraq's defeat, information about the ease with which Saddam Hussein had exploited the international arms market, and the embarrassing provenance of much of Iraq's weaponry, suggested to many that an unregulated or poorly regulated international arms market was not acceptable. One further lesson of the Iraqi arms build-up was that the transfer of weapon manufacturing technology, and particularly dual-use technology which can have both military and civilian applications, can over time prove to be as significant as transfers of completed weapons. The modern 'arms' trade therefore has to be understood as involving weapons of varying sophistication, tangible technology of both military and civil origin, and intangible 'know-how'.

A rush of declarations and initiatives followed the Iraqi defeat: the CSCE declarations of June 1991 and January 1992 and the subsequent publication in November 1993 of 'Principles and Guidelines Governing Conventional Arms Transfers'; the Group of Seven's 'Declaration on Conventional Arms Transfers and NBC Non-Proliferation' in July 1991; the announcement of the European Community's 'criteria' for arms exports in 1991 and 1992; the Permanent Five members of the Security Council and their 'Guidelines for Conventional Arms Transfers' in October 1991; the

UN's Conventional Arms Register launched in December 1991; the European Union 'dual-use' technology export control regulation established in July 1995; and the negotiations to replace the Co-ordinating Committee for Multilateral Export Controls from 1994 to 1996. By the summer of 1996, however, none of these initiatives had achieved much of note, if achievement is measured in terms of restraining the eagerness with which established arms suppliers exploit the international export market.

The object of this book is to describe the main features of the post-Cold War arms trade. While seeking explanations for some of the difficulties which have so far attended attempts to regulate or restrain the market, it is not the purpose of this book to offer apologies or excuses for any failures or shortcomings which have so far occurred. The central proposition of the book is that while the arms trade is a complex, international phenomenon, and while it is logical for states to wish to co-operate if regulation of the arms trade is to be effective, there is a powerful and persuasive element of particularism and nationalism which increasingly influences both participation in the arms trade and its regulation, and discussion of it. The arms trade is a phenomenon which may be understood and described on the international level, but could more appropriately be addressed, in terms of regulatory policy, at the national level. The international arms trade is a broad and complex affair, and one which frequently provokes heated debate and controversy. There are many possible approaches to the subject and, where it is relevant, the reader's attention will be drawn to alternative interpretations of the issue under discussion. To enable the reader to compensate for the author's preconceptions, it is as well to identify, from the outset, the assumptions and preconceptions from which this study proceeds. There are two such assumptions. First, the book is written – albeit not uncritically – largely from what theorists of modern international relations would call a 'classical realist', '*realpolitik*' or 'power politics' view of the way international political life is organized. This is neither the only, nor perhaps the most subtle way of describing the world; in recent years the realist school has itself tried to become rather more refined. But the three basic tenets of realist theory are particularly apposite for a study of the international arms trade. For the realist, the state is the dominant actor in the international system; it is clear that the international arms market is also largely a matter of relations between states and their governments, although the 'grey' and 'black' international arms markets tend to be organized somewhat less formally. In the realist canon, the state acknowledges no superior authority; we will come across the notion that the acquisition and possession of arms is an *inalienable* right of states, simply because they are states. Finally, states are held by realists to be predominantly interested in power, their own and that of other states; it will be argued here that a large part of the incentive to take part in and regulate the international arms trade springs from a sense that the arms trade is above all a matter of the distribution of raw, military *power*.

The second assumption is revealed in the book's stress on the supply-side of the international arms market. This is perhaps more of a choice than an assumption, but should nevertheless be explained. Analysts and government officials alike argue that there will be little progress in regulating the international arms trade until both suppliers and clients can be brought together under a common regulatory roof. This is a commendable enough aim, but it does of course take more than merit to make an objective attainable. On empirical grounds alone, the successful coming together of suppliers and clients appears unlikely. And as this study will try to show, the obstacles to supplier/recipient co-operation are becoming greater. This study therefore concentrates on the supply-side of the equation. This is not to say that the supply-side should be held to be the 'cause' of the arms trade, and should therefore be the exclusive focus of all efforts to control the market, although some commentators take precisely that view. Rather, the object is to ensure that the best does not become the enemy of the good. If effective co-operation between suppliers and recipients of conventional arms and technology is judged to be nothing more than a chimera, then its whole-hearted pursuit could amount to little more than a cynical excuse for inactivity among the suppliers.

Chapter 2 describes the dynamics of the post-Cold War international arms market. What is the size and scope of the market? Who are the main actors, on the supply-side as well as the demand-side? Is the supply/demand relationship altering? How is defence industry adapting to changing circumstances? What are the difficulties in controlling the trade? Chapter 3 examines the question of control in more detail, assessing the main rationales for control and the mechanisms – national and multilateral – which are currently available to regulate or supervise the export and traffic of conventional arms and related technology. Chapter 4 asks why it is so difficult to establish a central, universal code or set of principles by which to guide export control policies. Of particular interest here is the way in which multilateral control initiatives – especially those which derive their legitimacy from values which are understood or portrayed by the would-be controllers to be internationally acceptable – are viewed by customers in the international arms market, customers who are finding increasingly that the initiative in the market place is working to their advantage. Chapter 5 summarizes the discussion and offers some concluding comments.

2

MARKET FORCES

INTRODUCTION

One way to begin this description of the international arms market is to assert that, as with any other trading system, there must be a 'demand-side' (in this case countries wishing to buy weapons and military equipment), a 'supply-side' of countries able to manufacture and sell such goods, and some sort of commercial arrangement which allows the two sides to meet. But beyond this point, bold commercial and economic analogies cease to be of very much use on their own. The language of international commerce is often used to describe and analyse the arms trade, and in one sense the arms trade is indeed all about making, buying and selling. But there are also political and ethical dimensions of the arms trade which are not – and could not be – captured by a relatively straightforward commercial equation. Even a passing acquaintance with the domestic politics of, say, the Western liberal democracies would make clear that participation in the arms trade can be a rather highly charged issue.

Critics of the arms trade attack on two fronts. In the first place, they reject the idea that weapons are merely commodities, just like washing-machines, which have no innate political or moral significance; this is an objection which will be discussed more fully in Chapter 3. Critics also reject the notion of a disinterested, market-led relationship between producer and consumer, with arms-manufacturing governments and firms behaving with the passivity and innocence of a corner shopkeeper. They argue instead that the dissemination of a deliberately fabricated culture of mistrust and confrontation, as well as more direct 'market-creation' activities, both conspire to cultivate a demand for weapons (and perhaps even an arms race) which the suppliers – the so-called merchants of death – then fuel.

An alternative perspective is that, in present circumstances there are legitimate – and perhaps even good – reasons why arms should be made and sold. And it is neither reasonable nor useful to label all individuals involved in the manufacture and trade of weapons as either criminals or sinners, or both. A better way to begin, one which could encompass both the commercial and all these other, rather less tidy considerations, would be to ask why there is a market for weapons. Why do some states import, and others make and export, arms? Taking this rather broader approach, the detailed statistics regarding the size and dynamics of the international arms market, and the identity of the main suppliers and recipients, should fall more easily into place. Accordingly, this chapter begins by describing the size and dynamics of the international arms market and goes on to examine other key issues. How has defence industry adapted to the end of the Cold War? What are the main difficulties in controlling the international traffic in arms? For political, commercial and strategic reasons, arms sales and transfers between states are often shrouded in secrecy. But there are also sectors of the market in which the idea of openness and public accountability is unlikely to find much acknowledgement, however perfunctory; brief mention will be made of both the covert (or 'grey') and illegal (or 'black') international arms markets.

WHY DO STATES IMPORT ARMS?

There are many reasons why a state might wish to import arms and military equipment, and these can be grouped into two sets: external and internal. The two sets overlap. For example, perceptions of external military threat can be as much a product of national domestic politics as real and objective knowledge or experience of another state's aggressive intent. The acquisition of weapons and military equipment for domestic reasons could also suddenly and adversely affect the strategic calculations and risk-perceptions of neighbours.

External Considerations

External considerations are the customary starting point; it is often in the language of national sovereignty and self defence that arguments for the arms trade, both generally and for specific contracts, are made. Most governments around the world would argue that, even without a direct and tangible military threat, there is a duty placed on them to provide for the defence of their people, their property and the national interest. In a world where violence and war are commonplace – perhaps even inevitable – self-defence is seen to be vital. It may also be that communities of all types and sizes have a deep-seated, psychological need for security and protection, which they expect leaders and governments to provide; this would be another example of where the external and domestic agendas meet. Of course, the most powerful external factor, and justification for arms imports, is the emergence of a real, objective military threat. To state that Country A constitutes a military threat to Country B requires three conditions to be met. First, Country A must have the military *capability* to mount an attack of some sort. Second, Country A must demonstrate the *intention* to mount such an attack. Finally, Country B – that is to say, its borders and territory, economic and strategic interests, and even cultural values – must be perceived to be *vulnerable* to Country A. If all these conditions are met, Country B might be expected, if domestic resources are inadequate, to look to foreign suppliers to fill any deficiencies in its weaponry and military equipment. All this may be to state the obvious. But what this simple equation should demonstrate is that talk of 'real' and 'objective' military threats can be deceptive. Threat assessment is not only a matter of hard military intelligence as to the number of tanks held by Country A, their operational range and so forth, but also a matter of political judgement. Threat assessment is a complex and often highly subjective process, one which is open to disagreement, error and even manipulation. And decisions – such as about arms imports – which are based on threat assessments are consequently open to interpretation and challenge.

There is also a problem of timing; contracts to supply arms and military equipment can take many years to fill. Manufacturers and purchasers often look five, ten or even fifteen years into the future. For this reason, recourse to the international arms market is probably not the most sensible response to a sudden attack, such as that mounted by Iraq on Kuwait in August 1990. To the extent that more arms and military equipment can offer a solution to such crises, a more fitting response to a surprise attack – perhaps the only hope for the inadequately armed victim – might be to request urgent military aid and defence from friends and allies. In an age of highly accurate and timely satellite surveillance, Iraq's military build-up and surprise attack were probably exceptional events. But continuing developments in weapons technology – especially in missiles and 'stealth' combat aircraft which can evade radar detection – will ensure that sudden, unanticipated and possibly decisive attack remains a possibility. All this suggests that the rationale for arms imports may be at its weakest when the case for self-defence against aggression is most pressing. It would appear, therefore, that much of the rationale for what would be described as 'legitimate' and 'defensive' weapons purchases has more to do with longer-term political judgements and impressions, with the politics of 'what if?', 'worst case analysis' and 'contingency planning'. But with these types of thinking comes the risk that arms purchases based upon a maladroit judgement of a neighbour's future intent might develop into a self-fulfilling prophecy.

Internal Considerations

Internal considerations are rather more complex, not least because they involve the psychology of leaders and nations and the often arcane and unpredictable domestic affairs of states. A government which harbours aggressive intent towards its neighbours, or which plans to use armed force to suppress internal dissidence, might seek to acquire weapons on the international market or, more commonly, on the covert or illegal markets. An autocratic leader's martial self-image might also result in purchases of military equipment. Then there are arguments that access to top-range military equipment and technology provides a source of technology and know-how which can be used for general industrial development. These arguments are often heard, and just as often challenged (Mohammed, pp.51–54). Some defence and development economists argue that military spending in developing countries represents huge, unbearable burdens on fledgling national economies. There may be some 'spin-off' benefits for general economic development but these are marginal, and any benefits of military spending are far outweighed by the opportunity costs. Economic and industrial development is best addressed, the critics claim, by direct investment in civil industry, housing, infrastructure and so forth. However, if civil access to military technology is of questionable benefit generally to an economy, the presumption by suppliers that access to 'leading edge' or 'sensitive' technology should be denied, for strategic reasons, could also impose costs on developing countries. Particularly where technology can be classified as 'dual-use', with civilian and military applications, the need to ensure that the technology is being sought for non-aggressive purposes, and the need to have export control systems flexible enough to allow such legitimate uses, present difficult problems for those seeking ways to regulate the international trade in arms and technology. Over-cautious export controls run the risk of undermining development for the sake of security. An underdeveloped economy can lead to political instability, with the attendant security risks for neighbours, friends and allies.

Less contentious, if only as a rationale for weapons imports, is the argument that the acquisition of new weaponry and equipment can be a source of defence technology to enable the creation of indigenous defence industries. 'Reverse engineering' and 'copy-cat' reproduction of military equipment which has been bought, borrowed, captured or stolen, is not a new phenomenon; within weeks of the British air raid on the Ruhr dams in 1943, German military scientists had reverse engineered an unexploded 'bouncing bomb' and rapidly developed an improved version of the weapon. The modern equivalent is the demands made by purchasers for 'off-set' benefits to be included in the arms supplier's tender for contract. These can range from agreements to buy or manufacture key sub-components locally, to agreements to supply and install complete manufacturing plants on the recipient's territory. The consequence is that not only is a weapon exported, but also a good deal of manufacturing and development technology and 'know-how'.

WHY DO STATES EXPORT ARMS?

Various factors can influence the decision to export weapons and military equipment. One common argument is that defence industry, like any other sector, needs to export its goods to remain profitable and competitive. Defence industry can often be a large employer, and without exports many of the jobs it provides could be lost. Defence exports can also improve the balances of trade and payments and therefore be an important contributor to national economic performance. Income from exports can enable industry to keep down the unit costs of its products, making them more attractive domestically and on the international market. Export income can also, as in any other industries, be used to fund speculative research and development. But against these arguments must be set the view that defence industry and defence exports, no matter how lucrative and manpower-intensive, can also represent opportunity costs for the exporter's economy, just as they can be a burden on the recipient's economy. In other words, there could be better and more effective ways of making money and creating employment.

The Needs of Defence Industry

In the majority of arms manufacturing and exporting countries, defence industry and government enjoy a very close relationship. This results in part from the fact that national governments, as the exclusive source of legitimacy for the use of armed force nationally, and the main agent for the use of military force internationally on behalf of the United Nations or some other legitimizing body, are the sole or main customer for the products of defence industries. Another explanation is that governments are driven by a 'national security' mentality in their dealings with defence industry. More so than in any other industrial sector, defence industry can be seen as a vital national resource, a strategic asset rather like standing armed forces. By this view, a 'healthy defence industry', one which is therefore busy on the international market, is a legitimate and necessary goal of government. Even when peaceful conditions obtain, and external military threats are hardest to define, governments might see a lively defence industry as an essential part of the contingency planning process; future threats cannot be predicted, but neither can they be entirely discounted. Particularly as weapons and equipment have become more complex and technologically advanced, with long lead-times for research and development, an effective defence sector could not be recreated quickly once it had been allowed to decay. Governments might therefore be as wary of allowing arms manufacturing capacity to slip, as they would be wary of doing away with armed forces altogether. Something like this argument has been around since modern, heavily industrialised warfare came about, leading to the idea that defence industry – or industry generally – should have sufficient 'surge capacity' to produce enough high-quality weapons if and when war broke out, and avoid losing an 'arms race' with a more productive adversary. The modern equivalent, acknowledging the technologically advanced nature of modern weaponry, lies in the idea of 'design freeze' or 'develop and refrigerate'. Here, all aspects of the research, design, development and computer aided testing of a new weapon are carried out, leaving final production to take place only *in extremis*. There are some doubts as to the speed with which a frozen production line could be 'recovered' to produce reliable equipment, but the advocates of this 'virtual manufacturing' argue that, particularly with advanced computer aided design, even the most complex electronic and mechanical systems and configurations could be modelled and 'tested' reliably and accurately. Yet any research and development programme needs some source of funding, and since few if any firms could survive by producing blue-prints for products which might never be bought and deployed, there would still be a need to export weapons for straightforward commercial reasons. Alternatively, firms would have to apply to their national government for very large subsidies, a course which is unlikely to meet with success during times of peace and defence cutbacks.

Arms Exports and Foreign Policy

There is also a foreign policy argument to consider. As the British government has put it; 'Our foreign policy objectives can also be served through defence exports; by helping friends to defend themselves; promoting regional stability and international security; and fostering good bilateral relations' (House of Commons, p.6). It is, of course, one thing to say that arms exports can supplement and cement existing relationships between countries, but rather another to say either that arms exports can in some way be a substitute for foreign policy and be instrumental in their own right, or that an important goal of foreign policy should be to promote the export of arms. The entanglement of arms exports with foreign policy arouses particular controversy; if an arms-exporting state's 'friends' are simply those countries which buy its weapons, and if diplomats act as arms salesmen, this could prove to be a short-sighted policy which runs the risk of creating well-armed adversaries when regimes change. But, as the international arms market becomes more diffuse and competitive, the relationship between arms exports and foreign policy is in any case becoming more tenuous. In the past, when the production of modern, sophisticated weaponry was monopolized by a very small number of countries, it was relatively easy for those countries to maintain close links between arms exports and foreign policy. But the glut of old and new weapons suppliers in the post-Cold War world has resulted in a buyer's market, where customers can select from a variety of sources and can easily reject those which attach too many, or indeed any, conditions. In the face of such competition and unpredictability, foreign policy which was too closely identified with arms exports might prove to be too inflexible to be of much value.

Prisoner's Dilemma

There is, finally, the claim that 'if we don't export arms, others will.' This is not so much an argument for exporting, as an argument against not exporting. Why, the argument goes, should jobs, foreign earnings, and an important sector of national industrial life, be sacrificed to some vague and pious idea of self-restraint by one or a small group of suppliers, if competitors are willing, able and likely to exploit any market opportunities? There are those who feel that this argument lies at the heart of the failure so far to co-operate internationally in the regulation of the conventional arms market, and who see this argument undermining their view that arms exports – if and when they have to take place – should be the result of a positive choice, rather than peer group inertia. Some of the annoyance and frustration which this relativism engenders might be explained in terms of the 'Prisoner's Dilemma' game. This is the scene where two prisoners being interrogated in separate cells are told that if both co-operate and confess to the crime, each will receive a six year sentence. If both refuse, each receives a two year sentence. If one confesses but the other refuses, the former walks free and the latter receives a ten year sentence. Although it makes sense for each to place maximum trust in the other and refuse to co-operate, the prospect of freedom and the threat of being left with a ten year sentence mean that neither is willing to co-operate with the other, each confesses, and receives a sentence worse than if he had said nothing. As far as arms export controls are concerned, the argument can be put another way: 'Domestic economic interests argue that, where multiple sources exist, little is to be gained from unilateral restraint on sales' (Mussington, p.42).

THE SIZE OF THE INTERNATIONAL ARMS MARKET

There have been several attempts in the twentieth century to quantify the international arms market. There has, however, been little agreement as to the most appropriate device for measuring the movement of arms and military equipment around the world. This largely reflects the reluctance of governments to release information regarding weapons holdings and transfers, for predictable reasons of national security, loyalty to allies, commercial confidentiality, and a wish in some cases to avoid public censure. The idea that national security could be *enhanced* by releasing such information to a 'transparent' confidence-building system has taken many years to take hold, and is still rather fragile. Statistics on the international arms trade must be treated with a great deal of caution; not only do the various agencies involved have different objectives, they also use incompatible counting methods. As a result, the size of the arms trade is very often more a matter of debate than fact, and sets of data can often have unanticipated uses in diplomacy and domestic politics.

Counting Methods

The simplest counting method might be to record the *volume* of the trade: the quantities of tanks, ships, rifles and so forth which are traded. However, while this approach might have been reasonable enough as little as one hundred years ago, when weapons were more homogeneous in design and performance, and when the pace of military innovation was much slower than at present, it now begs so many questions that its value is doubtful. Should some attempt be made to distinguish between the 'weapon' (e.g., a missile) and the 'weapon platform' (e.g., a combat aircraft) which launches it? Should non-weapon equipment such as trucks and even uniforms be included? How can modernization be accounted for? 'Tank' could describe a wide variety of self-propelled, direct-fire, armoured vehicles. But, in military and technological terms, there is very little sense in which a 1990s model – with composite armour, a long-range turbo-diesel engine and a main gun capable of rapid-firing large-calibre kinetic energy ammunition – has the same value, militarily or commercially, as its 1950s predecessor which is, nevertheless, still in service in some armies. If qualitative considerations, such as strategic and tactical effectiveness, are the object of the assessment, how can these data be presented in a consistent, useful way? One answer might be to seek prior agreement on an international definition of 'tank', 'warship', 'missile' and so forth. This approach has been used with some success in the November 1990 Conventional Armed Forces in Europe (CFE) arms control treaty, and in the United Nations Register of Conventional Arms. But in the absence of a pressing need to achieve some desired objective, such as controlled disarmament, agreements of this sort do not come easily. Without continuing negotiation and comparison, such agreements can also fail to keep up with innovation and become outdated fairly quickly. Unscrupulous weapons manufacturers and traders might also exploit any grey areas between and on the edges of the accepted definitions; at what point does an 'armed reconnaissance' aircraft become a ground-attack fighter, for example?

The only passably objective denominator is the currency value of the transaction. As a result, the 'size' of the international arms trade is usually expressed in cash terms. For development economists, interested in the opportunity costs of military spending and arms imports, calculations of the value of arms deals are important tools. In a very basic way, monetary value can also be an indicator of military significance, since the military effectiveness of 'leading edge' weaponry and equipment is likely to be reflected in its cost. But there remain important discrepancies: which military sales should be included, should the value be calculated when the order is made or when the equipment is delivered, and how can alternative means of payment and 'off-set' arrangements be explained?

In the twentieth century, the first attempt at measuring the arms trade combined two counting methods: quantity and currency value. In 1924, the Council of the League of Nations decided to compile and publish periodical statistics on the international arms trade. States were called upon to provide the League Secretariat with the appropriate documentation. The *Statistical Year-Book of the League of Nations* (not to be confused with the *Armament Year-Book*, something more akin to the modern *Military Balance* published annually by the International Institute for Strategic Studies in London) was produced annually between 1925 and 1938. The Year-Book included various tables showing the import and export of weapons and ammunition by class, destination and origin, as well as the gold dollar value of the transactions. The series suffered, however, from incomplete statistical information and a failure to establish common criteria among the participating governments. The Year-Book also contained very little information on heavy weapons such as armour, artillery, aircraft and warships (SIPRI [1971], pp.93–4). After the Second World War, the idea of registering international arms transfers by quantity received more attention. From the mid-1960s onwards, a series of resolutions was passed by the General Assembly of the United Nations, calling for some form of 'transparency' system, by which arms transactions would be revealed to governments and publics. But it was not until the early 1990s that a new registration system came about in the form of the United Nations Conventional Arms Register, which is discussed in Chapter 3.

In spite of counting difficulties and inconsistencies, it is the currency value of arms transactions which is still held to be the most useful and accurate measuring tool. The three most widely publicized annual sets of statistics come from the US Arms Control and Disarmament Agency (ACDA), the Congressional Research Service (CRS), also in the United States, and the independent Stockholm International Peace Research Institute (SIPRI).

ACDA tables refer to the exports and imports of almost 150 countries. These countries are also grouped into various sets, such as the membership of NATO and OPEC. Using official US government trade and defence statistics and 'estimates by US government sources' – an expression which is usually assumed to refer to US intelligence material – ACDA track the movement of a vast array of military equipment. The commodities under scrutiny range from guided missiles to small-arms, ammunition, uniforms and parachutes and, where relevant, 'dual-use'(i.e., civil/military) equipment. ACDA also accounts for the construction of arms factories when they are part of the transaction. ACDA's primary measuring device is the cash value (in US dollars) of transactions. In recent years, however, ACDA has also begun to provide a cautious analysis of the quantities of weapons delivered to developing countries in four main categories: land armaments, naval craft, aircraft and missiles. Using, once again, 'US government sources', the CRS publication calculates the value of all arms transfer agreements with the Third World, as well as the value of actual deliveries by calendar year. 'Third World' is defined as all countries except the United States, Canada, the former Soviet Union, Europe, Japan, Australia and New Zealand. Most categories of major weapons and weapon platforms are included, but the CRS coverage is narrower than that provided by ACDA. Apart from non-combat military aircraft, the CRS tables do not account for sales of support and logistic equipment or defence-related infrastructure, and do not record sales of small arms and small-calibre mortars. Like ACDA, the CRS publication also lists the quantities of the various weapons delivered by 'major suppliers' to Third World destinations.

SIPRI, the third main source of statistics, relies upon openly published – or at least attributable – data and examines world-wide transactions under six categories: aircraft, armoured vehicles, artillery, guidance and radar systems, missiles and warships. SIPRI statistics do not include the trade in small arms, small calibre artillery and mortars, ammunition, support equipment, services and components or production technology. SIPRI argues that 'publicly available information is inadequate to track these items satisfactorily.'[1] Providing more detailed information than ACDA and CRS, SIPRI does however list the suppliers and recipients of major weapons, the number ordered, the weapon designation (e.g., 'AIM-9S Sidewinder'), the description of the weapon (e.g., 'air-to-air missile'), the years of orders and deliveries and the numbers so far delivered or produced, and adds comments such as the intended user, leasing arrangements and the equipment to be upgraded. In order to provide a means by which to compare national involvement in the arms trade, SIPRI also expresses transactions in terms of 'trend-indicator values'. SIPRI's object is to establish the important trends in regional activity, supply and demand relationships and so forth, rather than record in strict and real terms the values of arms transactions. SIPRI considers the available financial information to be too unreliable. Some information is simply not available, in some cases the price paid may vary considerably, and then there are grants, gifts, barter and other 'off-set' arrangements to consider. Thus, when SIPRI describes the world trade in major conventional weapons in terms of US dollars, and provides a figure for 1994 of US$21,725 million (at constant 1990 prices), this is a trend-indicator value rather than a real 'market' value.

SIPRI's counting method is certainly the most elaborate, but the SIPRI statistics are most commonly available and probably the most widely read. It is perhaps not surprising, therefore, that misunderstandings frequently occur when SIPRI figures are cited. A country's arms export performance can be an important source of domestic political capital and can provide a foundation for further export contracts. Thus, early in 1993 Britain's defence procurement minister claimed proudly that British 'defence exports' in 1992 had amounted to £4.5 billion, or a remarkable 20 per cent of the world market[2] – an assessment with which ACDA was later in broad agreement (see Figure 3). Later that year, however, when SIPRI's calculations for 1992 were published, a conflicting message was given with the UK shown to have exported a mere US$952 million, or just over 5 per cent of the world total. More significantly perhaps, for the UK government's domestic political image and its perceived strengths as an arms exporter, the UK was shown to have performed less well than France, Germany and the People's Republic of China. (SIPRI [1993], p.444). The British government uses a completely different counting system which includes all military contracts (and is therefore more akin to the ACDA approach) and which is based on the real, market value of the contract when signed.

If governments can be embarrassed or annoyed by too little publicity, they can also take exception to too much exposure. The 1994 CRS report placed France as the leading supplier of conventional weapons to the Third World, supplanting the United States for the first time. The French government responded with 'extreme irritation', accusing the CRS report of attempting to invigorate US arms manufacturers to make greater efforts at exports, and of planting 'the idea that France, in addition to letting off nuclear weapons in the South Pacific, is unscrupulously peddling arms to Third World regimes.'[3]

The Size of the Market

In spite of the difficulties – and occasionally controversies – which attend the business of measuring the global arms trade, there is general agreement that the market has contracted dramatically since the late 1980s. ACDA record that by 1993 – the latest year for they have published figures – the world market had fallen to approximately US$22 billion. This represents a fall of some 70 per cent from the 1987 figure of over US$74 billion, and places the size of the market at the level of the early 1970s. (ACDA, p.9). The rate of contraction seems to be slowing, suggesting that the world market could stabilize around the figure of US$20 billion. Figure 1 illustrates the decline in the size of the world market from the 1987 peak, from both the ACDA and the SIPRI points of view.

THE INTERNATIONAL ARMS MARKET 1985-93

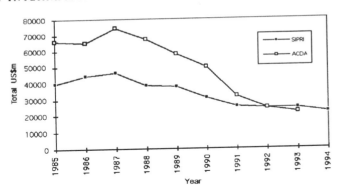

FIGURE 1. SOURCES: SIPRI *YEARBOOK* 1995 P.511; ACDA, *WMEAT* 1993-1994, P.91

The Buyers

Saudi Arabia heads ACDA's list of arms importers, having imported some US$5.1 billion worth of arms in 1993. Next on the list come the United States, Egypt, Iran and Turkey, all at around one billion US dollars. Developing countries took approximately 78 per cent (or US$17 billion) of the market in 1993. For 1993, the busiest importing region in the world continued to be the Middle East, accounting for about 43 per cent of the world market (see Figure 2). A common impression of the situation in the Middle East is of a series of arms races over recent decades, with a sharp rise in spending since the mid-1980s, and a dramatic boost following the 1991 Gulf War and the demonstrations of advanced Western equipment. Britain has for the last decade been committed to massive arms deals in the region, particularly with Saudi Arabia through the Al Yamamah deal worth about £20 billion. Britain is facing stiff competition throughout the region, particularly from France and the United States. But there have been increasing signs that the Middle East is no longer the arms exporter's gold-mine it once was. The level of spending on military imports is still huge, and there is no doubt that, from a defence industrial point of view, the region is still a vital market. But by late 1994 there were reports of a shift towards upgrades of equipment rather than new, off-the-shelf purchases of the latest weaponry. And there were even suggestions that many buyers had overstretched themselves and were about to default on payments. By one view, the strategic balance in the region has now become so stable that 'the race for conventional military superiority has come to an end' (Karp, p.29). But the same writer cautions against complacency, warning that 'greater competition in weapons of mass destruction and long-range missiles remains likely' (Karp, p.44).

ACDA ranks East Asia as the third largest arms market; well behind the Middle East, but much closer behind Western Europe. For

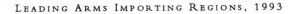

LEADING ARMS IMPORTING REGIONS, 1993

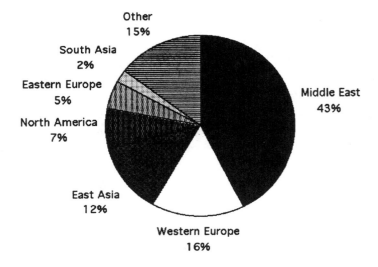

FIGURE 2. SOURCE: ACDA, *WMEAT* 1993–1994, P.9

surviving European and North American defence firms, keen to export their wares, the Pacific Rim and Southeast Asia are therefore of growing interest. Ambitious military spending plans in the region, combined with a readiness to export weapons to potential clients, have given rise to fears that an arms race has been set in motion in the Far East. With so many simmering tensions in the region – the Korean Peninsula, China and Taiwan, the Kurile Islands, the Paracel Islands and the Natuna Islands to name but a few – there is a grave danger that irresponsible behaviour by Western defence industries and governments could shatter the fragile strategic balance in the region. But the existence or otherwise of an arms race in the region has prompted steady debate in academic circles and the media in recent years. There is a persuasive school of thought which argues that 'arms race' is neither the most accurate, nor the most helpful description of what is taking place. An arms race could be described as a competition between two or more states to acquire sophisticated weaponry and military technology, in order not to be left at a strategic disadvantage. There is a sense, therefore, in which an arms race is an action–reaction dynamic. Yet for some analysts this is precisely what is missing in the case of the Far East; 'There are few unambiguous cases of particular acquisitions in one country leading to either imitative or offsetting acquisitions by other' (Ball, p.94). Instead, what could be taking place is a process of 'force modernization' across the region. With the departure of the United States from Southeast Asia and with uncertainty regarding the future of the US commitment to the wider Pacific area, some states feel uncomfortably exposed and hostage to the good intentions of the region's great military powers. The end of communist insurgency campaigns has also enabled many states to turn away from large-scale internal security concerns and focus instead on more traditional military tasks such as facing external threats, protecting Exclusive Economic Zones and fishing rights, gathering intelligence about their neighbours and even contributing to UN-sponsored peacekeeping operations.

The Sellers

The world's leading arms supplier in 1993 remained the United States, a position it has held since the early 1990s following the decline of its main single competitor, the Soviet Union. In 1993 the United States had a 47 per cent share of the world market (US$10.3 billion), with a further 28 per cent going collectively to the three main European suppliers (Great Britain, Germany and France, see Figure 3). The United Kingdom was ranked second overall, with nearly 20 per cent of the world market, and Russia third with 12 per cent. The Permanent Five members of the UN Security Council (the United States, Russia, China, France and

LEADING ARMS EXPORTERS, 1993

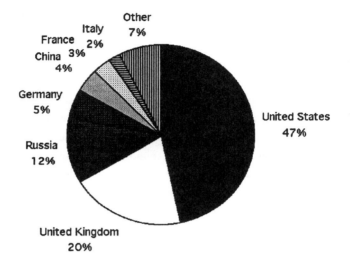

FIGURE 3. SOURCE: ACDA *WMEAT* 1993–1994, P.16

Great Britain) were responsible for about 86 per cent of arms exports in 1993. The developed world's arms exporters took a 92 per cent share of the market in 1993. 'Developing country exporters' (China, Israel, Spain, North Korea, Brazil, Bulgaria, South Korea and Egypt) had what ACDA describes as a 'fairly stable' share of the market, at around ten per cent. World market shares could alter dramatically if and when the Russian defence industry mounts its long-awaited export drive and regains some of the share lost with the end of the Cold War and the collapse of the Soviet Union. Increased marketing activity by the Russians was apparent in early 1996, with the possibility of Russian participation in manufacturing joint ventures and sales of weapons, ammunition and equipment to Brazil, India, Myanmar, the Philippines and Vietnam, as well as several other potential clients.

ARMS TRADE DYNAMICS

The post-Cold War arms market is clearly, at least for the present, dominated by a small group of developed world suppliers. Furthermore, within this group, it is a handful of North American and Western European suppliers which lead the market. Although some traditional, Cold War-style patterns of supply and demand remain, the predominance of these Western suppliers gives the first indication that the international arms market has changed fundamentally with the ending of the Cold War.

Smaller and Looser

The end of the Cold War brought with it the collapse of a major source of arms – the Soviet Union – with which Western suppliers would no longer have to compete in the world market. Yet the end of the Cold War also meant reduced emphasis in the West and elsewhere on defence and on the need for large-scale military spending and timely procurement of arms and military equipment; the cash value of the world market has, as shown above in Figure 1, shrunk dramatically. The end of the Cold War therefore had, and continues to have, a depressing effect on Western defence industries, resulting in the 'downsizing' and restructuring of defence industrial sectors and increased interest in defence exports, albeit into a much reduced market. But what also disappeared with the passing of the Cold War was the adversarial relationship which underpinned much arms export activity and which, arguably, not only boosted the market but also did a great deal to shape, direct and regulate it. After the Cold War, the notion of the world divided into 'spheres of influence', reflecting the ideological rivalry of the Cold War, could no longer provide an adequate explanation of the dynamics of arms supply and demand. It might therefore be thought that reduced defence spending domestically and around the world could be counter-balanced by a looser political framework, in which those arms producers able to remain in business would enjoy more varied commercial opportunities by selling, for example, to states which had previously been clients of Cold War adversaries. But explanations of the post-Cold War arms market which confine themselves to Cold War terms of reference overlook or misunderstand the dynamics of the post-Cold War arms trade. These new dynamics, all interconnected, include the initiative and market strength which is now enjoyed by the demand side, the spread of manufacturing capability, and the 'civilianization' of technological innovation and military development.

Manufacturing Overcapacity

European and North American defence manufacturers in particular have been adjusting to the reduced demand for arms after the Cold War by downsizing, merging and in some cases by leaving defence manufacturing altogether. But why is it that the stable, qualitatively superior weapons manufacturers which remain have not been able jointly to enjoy their near-monopoly position in a market which, albeit clearly reduced in size, has also been opened up by the removal of ideological barriers to trade? If the West can be said to have 'won' the Cold War, why can it not be said to have 'won' the international arms trade? The explanation is that the contraction in the supply-side has been accompanied, and off-set, by a much more dramatic contraction in the size of the world market as a whole. There remains, even after all the defence industrial restructuring which has so far taken place, a massive excess in supply over conceivable demand. In these circumstances, the advantage in the market-place has shifted steadily from the producer to the buyer, and defence contracts have become the subject of ever more vigorous competition. Western and developed-world defence industries, and the governments which sponsor them, have had to compete among themselves for the defence contracts that remain. It is as if the ideological or vertical competitiveness of the Cold War arms trade has been replaced by a more straightforward commercialism which operates horizontally and globally. What is more, it may be unwise to write ideology out of the framework altogether; as Chapter 4 will suggest, growing divisions between the developed and the developing worlds, exemplified by the so-called clash of civilizations and similar ideas, may amount to a conceptual stiffening of the stronger position in the market-place now enjoyed by the demand side. But this chapter turns now to another important aspect of defence industry's activities after the Cold War – the 'internationalization' of defence production, which again contributes to a market which is more diffused, less predictable and less controllable.

INTERNATIONALIZATION AND DIFFUSION OF DEFENCE INDUSTRY

The pursuit of foreign partners and subsidiaries is not unique to defence industries; it is normal practice in manufacturing industry to seek foreign connections in order to share costs and reduce risks, gain access to foreign innovation, achieve economies of scale and penetrate foreign markets. When domestic economic conditions are unfavourable and commercial risks are high, the pressure to seek international partners can be very intense. Joint ventures and international mergers can take place on a national, regional and even world-wide scale. In some cases, defence companies have been tempted to shift whole sectors of their production cycle to developing regions in order to take advantage of cheaper labour and production costs and unrivalled expertise in the manufacture of certain key sub-components such as semi-conductors. This process, known as 'off-shoring', has been especially noticeable in the 1990s. Often, the chosen site has been in the Asia–Pacific region and South-East Asia, with Taiwan, Indonesia, South Korea and Singapore being particularly favoured (Willett, p.115).

As the process of internationalization leads to the establishment of cross-border joint venture companies and international project consortia, so some damage is done to the highly protective 'national security' mentality through which defence industry has traditionally been perceived. What is more, when it comes to exercising control over arms manufacturing and exporting, difficult questions arise as to the ownership and legal status of these industrial bodies; who – or what – is responsible to whom for compliance with export controls and guidelines? At what level of political authority should such controls and guidelines be issued? Could such bodies make it possible to evade national and multilateral export policies and restrictions? Or could they simply make the task of export control, nationally and regionally, more difficult than it would otherwise be? There is already some evidence to suggest that the export of multinationally–produced defence equipment causes difficulty for national and multilateral export control systems, even for relatively anodyne international initiatives such as the United Nations Register of Conventional Arms. One account of the process of cross-border mergers in Europe, for example, suggests that governmental influence upon industry is already diminishing, with defence companies 'following the directives of the authorities less and less' (Sandström and Wilén, pp.66,72). But other analysts argue that large multinational defence companies are not inherently more difficult to control than smaller companies. After all, every trading company has to be registered somewhere, and when it does so it comes under a national jurisdiction. Larger firms may, in addition, be more anxious to understand and comply with all relevant export control regulations, simply because they have more to lose in the event of misunderstandings or wilful non-compliance (Hofhansel, p.397). Most legitimate exporters of weapons and sensitive technology appear to accept that the international defence market is not an unregulated bonanza and that exports should conform to national practices and to nationally–implemented multilateral agreements. In any case, the gradual assumption of extra-territorial powers by governments, particularly in the United States and Europe, may make it easier for authorities in arms-producing states to extend the scope of their control and influence.

Off-Sets and Technology Transfers

A key feature of internationalization is the transfer of defence-related technology. Internationalization can involve the direct sale or release of manufacturing technology and skills. Technology transfers can also take place in other ways, as part of off-set arrangements in arms transfer deals, for example. Internationalization and technology transfers create new competitors and could, ultimately, be contrary to the interests of those industries which indulge in such practices. But in most cases defence industries, which cannot afford to overlook the export market, have to accept the diffusion of their knowledge and skills which participation in the international arms market unavoidably entails. As part of the process of competitive tendering for the supply of arms and military equipment, most buyers now demand in addition the transfer of manufacturing technology in the form of direct technology transfers, sub-contracting deals, licensed and co-development, and co-production. Although, as the ACDA figures indicate, most production still takes place among the traditional 'first tier' of weapons suppliers, the result of internationalization, through off-sets and the like, is that a significant 'second tier' as well as a less important 'third tier' of weapons producers have now developed (Anthony [1993], p.380). Off-sets commonly involve an agreement by the supplier to co-produce the weapon or its parts with the recipient country and, in time, even to license full production. Given the decline in domestic markets and the creation of a more open, world-wide 'buyer's market' for arms, off-set demands are becoming increasingly difficult to resist. A good example of the spread of technology through off-set deals is the South Korean purchase of General Dynamics F-16 fighters from the United States. This agreement involved the purchase of 12 aircraft direct from the United States, the assembly of a further 36 from production kits prepared in Fort Worth, Texas, and construction of the remaining 72 by Samsung Industries in Seoul. But perhaps the best known are the arrangements made between Saudi Arabia and various arms and technology suppliers. In the 1980s Saudi Arabia signed deals with the United States, Britain and France which involved the transfer of technology and know-how. The 'primary goal' of Saudi Arabia's off-set programme was described in stark and frank terms by one analyst as 'self-sufficiency in the high technology civil and, where feasible, defence industrial sectors.'[4]

More broadly, the spread of the ability to manufacture conventional weapons, and the arrival on the scene of a number of small but perfectly formed arms and technology suppliers, able to dominate niches in the international market and to supply the so-called pariah regimes such as Iran, Iraq, Libya and North Korea, suggest that the management of key parts of the international arms trade may now have moved beyond the control of any one government or of any small group of supplier governments, even where those governments agree to act completely in concert. When acting in a fully co-ordinated manner, supplier groups might be able to manage their own sector of the international market but probably ought not to expect to manage the market as a whole. The difficulty is that, once this limitation is perceived, it feeds back to and undermines the very notion of limited supply-side co-ordination, and reinforces the argument 'if we don't export, others will. ' In these circumstances, the best that might be expected is some form of 'transparency', or confidence-building measure, of the sort offered by the UN Conventional Arms Register, if and when it is expanded to include domestic procurement and weapons production.

The internationalization of defence industry, and the transfer by various means of weapons-related manufacturing technology, are important characteristics of the post-Cold War arms trade. They suggest both that the market domination achieved by a handful of suppliers will be increasingly challenged, and that the size of market share enjoyed by one or a small number of suppliers will have little bearing on the degree to which the international market can be controlled. Unless governments exercise extra-territorial powers systematically and effectively, a defence company may be British in name but may have little or no responsibility to British authorities. A third consideration, which again both defines the post-Cold War arms market and explains why it is becoming so difficult to regulate, is what might be called the 'civilianization' of technological innovation.

THE CIVILIANIZATION OF STRATEGIC TECHNOLOGY

The strategic impact of new military technology is a subject of endless fascination. Descriptions of new weaponry and military capability often refer to film footage of super-accurate cruise missiles 'turning left' at road junctions in Baghdad during the 1991 bombardment, and of precision-guided munitions flying down ventilation shafts; there can be no doubt that the technological sophistication of modern weaponry is increasing at a rapid rate. Among the projects allegedly running in Western defence research laboratories at present, the development of nano-circuitry and the possibility of micro-robot 'soldier ants' are particularly striking (Shukman, p.193). The thirst for sophisticated military equipment is spreading around the world. Some advocates of the technology-based, so-called Revolution in Military Affairs see the current phase of military innovation as heralding a new era in military technology and strategy. An alternative view is that the current 'revolution' is no more than the latest phase in a period of continuous and rapid development which began in the mid-nineteenth century and which looks set to continue (Buzan, p.27).

Who Owns Science?

The origins, duration and strategic impact of modern military technological innovation are of less interest here than the implications for attempts to control the rate and scope of technological diffusion. If export control policies are based upon the relatively simple premise that key technology can be 'owned', and denied to outsiders, are these policies any longer credible? Is it possible for the most advanced industrial nations to maintain the leading edge in military technology? The first problem which industrialized governments confront in this regard is the increasing difficulty of distinguishing between civilian and military technological development and application. The notion of 'spin-off' has been familiar since the 1950s; military research laboratories consumed vast sums for research and development and, occasionally, an application emerged which could have innocent civilian use. The development of Teflon for non-stick saucepans is often used to illustrate this phenomenon, although Teflon (polytetrafluoroethylene) was in fact discovered accidentally in a civilian laboratory in 1938. But during the 1970s and 1980s the 'direction of dependence' began to change and innovation began to flow from the commercial to the military sector, 'a trajectory characterized by spin-on rather than spin-off' (Willett, p.116). In some cases, leading-edge civilian firms have moved 'horizontally' into the defence sector, thus adding to the pressure on already beleaguered defence industries. The civilianization of leading-edge technological development is becoming so marked that the expression 'dual-use technology' is losing the precision it may once have had and is coming to mean nothing more than 'technology' itself. In some cases, the distinction between civil and military is deliberately blurred, as in the US 'Technology Reinvestment Project' which seeks out for special funding those military research projects which can have civilian applications. The US programme has led, for example, to military Global Positioning Satellite locating devices being used in family cars, and combat fighter software being used in the entertainment industry. Other examples of civilian use of military-related technology and equipment include image-intensifying and infra-red night vision and surveillance devices, data compression for rapid image and information transmission, lasers, mine detection, and obstacle avoidance alarms for helicopter pilots.

The civilianization and commercialization of technological innovation implies a diminution of government control over strategically significant research and development. Particularly in liberal, free market democracies, the scope for government control of commercial research is already limited. What is more, as technological capability spreads around the world, more states are becoming highly competent on or just behind the leading edge, even to the extent of dominating important niches such as semi-conductors. The commodities being traded are also changing. There is now much more interest in trading spare parts, components and upgrade packages, to the extent that the transfer of technology has become more important strategically and economically than completed weapons platforms (Neuman, p.64). As trade becomes more technology-based, as technology increasingly has both civil and military applications, and as technological diffusion occurs by 'intangible' means, or in the mind of a scientist, so the trade is becoming 'almost impossible to control' (Laurance [1992], p.167). If technology denial policies are becoming difficult, there are also arguments to suggest that they are unfair. Restricted access to those 'bronze medal technologies' which have become part of 'modern industrial and silicon society' could condemn some states to 'third class industrialization and a perpetually lower standard of living' (Zimmerman, p.82). Almost thirty years ago, D.S. Landes forecast some of the practical and political problems which could attend policies of technology denial:

> The one ingredient of modernization that is just about indispensable is technological maturity and the industrialization that goes with it; otherwise one has the trappings without the substance, the pretence without the reality. [...] This world, which has never before been ready to universally accept any of the universal faiths offered for its salvation, is apparently prepared to embrace the religion of science and technology without reservation (Landes, pp.7, 554).

For all these reasons, technology denial and export control policies face an uphill struggle. If technology denial is applied unwisely the effect could be to drive thwarted clients down the path of developing and deploying weapons covertly, perhaps even to investigate weapons of mass destruction. One response could be to focus upon those special, extremely sensitive technologies such as 'stealth', which could give decisive strategic advantage. But even here, for as long as it is possible to fight wars with second- or third-rate weapons, and even with basic agricultural implements, then any obsession with leading-edge weaponry could prove misplaced, perhaps dangerously so. The developed world could find itself equipped more and more with elaborate, highly integrated and extremely powerful military arsenals, but wholly ill-equipped to deal with low-level conflict breaking out around the world. If, in spite of these reservations, technology denial and export control remain the preferred responses, there is another fundamental decision to be made. Should the focus of a denial policy be upon the qualities of the machine or technology and its potential 'end-use', or upon the intentions and reputation of the 'end-user' destination? This is a dilemma which surfaces frequently during discussion of multilateral arms and technology trade regulation after the Cold War.

The pursuit of foreign industrial partners, the willingness to transfer technology through off-sets, and the changing dynamics of technological innovation, all create difficulties for the various export control initiatives discussed in the following chapter. But if these 'official' lines of supply create problems, so too does the 'semi-formal', 'grey market' where renegade arms importers and exporters are active. Some arms and technology transfers also take place in a 'black', covert and wholly unregulated international arms market.

THE GREY AND BLACK ARMS MARKETS

Often, states appear determined to acquire an arms manufacturing capability in the face of the harshest commercial, economic and political logic. This points to an obvious, but important, feature of the spread of arms manufacturing capabilities around the world; the spread is the result both of supplier industry 'push' and recipient 'pull'. The indigenization of weapons production capability is motivated in part by some of the internal considerations which drive arms imports, and in part by the perception that arms manufacturing is an inalienable attribute of a sovereign state, and proof of its political and military maturity. But rather than attempt to build up an arms industry from nothing, a goal which would require decades of industrial and scientific development to be compressed into a few years, states – as has been shown – instead demand off-set arrangements in order to ensure the rapid acquisition of the necessary technology and skills.

Self-sufficiency in arms manufacturing results not only from the transfer of technology through off-sets, however. Inconsistent policies or over-zealous export controls and embargoes can also play a part. Israel's response to the fickle behaviour of its arms suppliers was both to seek a variety of suppliers, in order to reduce dependence on any one, and, from the mid-1950s, to develop its own defence sector. Israel has never achieved self-sufficiency in its arms industry, but certainly became a considerable exporter during the 1980s. ACDA ranks Israel as the tenth largest arms exporter overall for 1993 and according to Israel's own estimates, some US$1,500 million worth of arms and equipment were exported in 1989 (ACDA, p.31; Anthony [1991], p.86). Defence industrial self-sufficiency was, however, achieved by South Africa. After the wholly ineffective non-mandatory embargo imposed in 1963, in November 1977 the United Nations Security Council imposed its first ever mandatory arms embargo on South Africa, prohibiting the supply of defence equipment to that country. According to one assessment, 'The arms embargo ... obliged South Africa's defence industry to become largely self-sufficient in providing military equipment for the [South African Defence Force] .. By the late 1980s the domestic defence industry had acquired across-the-board production capabilities and was able to supply the SADF with the bulk of its equipment needs.' Clandestine measures were often used to acquire key technologies, and some firms evaded the embargo by using South African subsidiaries. South Africa's arms industry flourished and South Africa became a major arms exporter in its own right, especially to fellow 'pariah' states and regimes (Batchelor and Willett, pp.5-6). The failure of the embargo to suppress South African defence acquisitions and manufacturing is demonstrated by the fact that in December 1984 the UN Security Council found it necessary to adopt Resolution 558, by which the purchase by United Nations members of South African arms, ammunition and military equipment was banned.

It is widely acknowledged that significant transfers of weapons and related technology have taken place covertly. Arms export scandals of one sort or another seem almost an occupational hazard for states and governments on the supply-side of the arms market. Chapter 3 will outline the case of the British defence firm Matrix Churchill, and the outcome of the subsequent inquiry ordered by the government. Covert transfers include those which are illegal, when international embargoes and national licensing procedures are circumvented, and those which are official, but not admitted. With transparency initiatives such as the UN Conventional Arms Register, and the efforts of independent bodies such as SIPRI, it is increasingly difficult to keep 'grey market' transactions out of the public eye. But it is not easy to speak with such confidence about the 'black market', where the uncontrolled and unobserved movement of modest quantities of ammunition and weapons can have disastrous consequences. It is one thing to keep track of consignments of large weapons systems such as ships, submarines and even armoured vehicles, through satellite observation and other means, but when the weapons being transferred illicitly are small in size (such as rifles, machine-guns, mortars and land-mines), effective monitoring is made doubly difficult.

The size of the illegal arms market is very difficult – if not impossible – to gauge with much accuracy. One estimate suggests that the size of the market could range from US$1 billion to as much as US$10 billion (about half as much again as the 'legal' arms trade), when demand is at its highest.[5] The size and consequences of 'black market' trading ought not to be underestimated, but the challenges which it represents seem more to do with prohibition and policing, and perhaps with the integrity of some governments. There is an argument that general participation in the UN Conventional Arms Register transparency exercise could have the indirect effect of exposing covert arms transactions. Indeed, discussion of the covert arms trade formed an important part of the process leading to the establishment of the Register in December 1991 (UN, paras 135-145). Subsequently, the UN General Assembly passed a series of resolutions aimed at drawing attention to the problem, particularly as it relates to terrorism and drug trafficking. The covert arms trade has also been discussed, albeit with little effect, at the UN Disarmament Commission, the 'deliberative organ' of the UN General Assembly where arms control and disarmament issues are concerned. The UNDC meets for four weeks each spring and makes a report to the General Assembly when it meets in the autumn. But so far, the general thrust of discussion has been that covert arms transfers are best tackled by improved policing, customs procedures and so forth. Rather than look to a complex international control regime, the emphasis has been on improving national efforts to combat the trade, while stressing the need for co-operation between governments, for example in the exchange of intelligence.

CONCLUSION

The international arms market has shrunk considerably in recent years. But at the same time, the market has become more diffuse and competitive. With transfers of strategically important technology proceeding briskly, and with military innovation increasingly coming about as a result of civilian research, the market must be expected to become looser still. As a result, what remains of the international market for arms and military technology is much less predictable and controllable. A 'world government', properly constituted and with real powers of enforcement, could manage and restrain such a market. But there is no such body, and the United Nations is at best a blurred outline of what might be achieved. A few Western suppliers dominate the market. But even if these suppliers could agree on goals and methods – which they cannot – and accept the penalties of self-restraint, a substantial (and growing) part of the international market would remain beyond their control.

NOTES

1. A full explanation of SIPRI's methodology can be found in a SIPRI Fact Sheet published in January 1995.
2. 'Arms sales on course for record', *The Times*, 10 February 1993.
3. 'French fury at figures in arms sales report', *Jane's Defence Weekly*, 19 August 1995.
4. 'Offsets: taking a strategic view', *Jane's Defence Weekly*, 5 February 1994.
5. 'The covert arms trade', *The Economist*, 12 February 1994.

3

CONTROLLING THE MARKET – MOTIVES AND MEANS

INTRODUCTION

In spite of the many obstacles in the way of effective control, some of which have been described in Chapter 2, the period between 1945 and the end of the Cold War saw the main arms-exporting governments in Western Europe and North America follow a 'trend towards government control of arms exports' which had been developing in the inter-war years (Krause, p.73). In the 1990s it may seem obvious that governments should wish to supervise and regulate the arms trade, and historically it has been the norm for governments to do so. Throughout history there have been attempts to stem the flow of newly developed arms and of military technology, because they were thought to be strategically crucial or because their use and effect seemed especially repugnant, or more often a little of both: the Greek ban on the Roman short sword, the prohibition on cross-bows ordered by the Second Lateran Council in 1139, French condemnation of the long-bow in the fourteenth century, unease about the introduction of the machine-gun in the nineteenth century, and in the first years of the twentieth century the British Admiralty's view of the submarine as a cowardly weapon. More recently, however, particularly in the late nineteenth century and in the years before the First World War, some governments have dallied with a *laisser-faire* approach to the arms trade. This is best seen as an exception to the general rule (Harkavy, p.213; Krause, p.61), but there are still occasional voices to be heard arguing that the international arms market is like any other commercial sector and should not therefore be subject to extraordinary intervention by governments.

Regulation of the arms trade has been the norm, or at least the aspiration. Regulatory efforts have been both formal and informal, ranging from arms trade embargoes to transparency initiatives. Activity has also taken place on many levels, from the United Nations down to *ad hoc* co-operation among governments. At the bottom of this pyramid of activity is the development of humble national export controls without which, arguably, none of the larger multilateral initiatives could have been attempted. This chapter asks why there is so much interest in regulating the arms trade; what is the rationale for arms and technology export control systems at both the national and the multilateral levels? The chapter then describes the evolution and structure of a typical national system, and finally examines the main post-Cold War efforts at multilateral regulation.

THE RATIONALE FOR NATIONAL REGULATION

Many of the proposals to regulate or reduce the international arms trade are guided by a sense of what would be best for the international community, or humanity itself. But it can equally be an unsentimental sense of protecting or advancing national interest which lies at the heart of efforts to manage the arms trade. National interest is an expression which is often used, but surprisingly difficult to define succinctly. Nevertheless, it is frequently in the name of this vague idea that governments collaborate in order more effectively to manage and supervise the international arms trade. For the purposes of this book, 'national interest' can be understood as a collection of pragmatic, legal and ethical ideas.

Pragmatic Politics

The pragmatist might see that for as long as there has been a demand for weapons and military equipment there has also been interest in the conduct and consequences of any transactions, with regular intervention in the market-place by those responsible for the production and supply of relevant goods and technology. Intervention in the arms trade is, as indicated above, hardly a new idea. The essential quality of defence-related trade, which underpins most assessments of the economic, political, technological and strategic implications of a given transaction, and which drives governments and authorities to intervene, is that the trade involves the distribution of military power. By extension, the defence and even survival of governments, states and societies could be affected; 'trade in armaments ... [has] potential to affect a nation's security [assuring] its treatment as a phenomenon uniquely relevant to world politics' (Laurance [1992], p.4). The pragmatist's perspective, therefore, amounts to the claim that it must be in the interest of all governments to avoid possible adverse consequences of defence-related trade by controlling the trade and the market-place.

International Law

As far as the legal dimensions of proliferation and arms exports are concerned, national governments are required under international law to have the means to supervise and regulate the arms trade. In some circumstances, unregulated arms sales and transfers could result in illegal intervention or even outright aggression. Since states have agreed, in the United Nations Charter and in various Security Council and General Assembly resolutions, to uphold the idea of the sovereign state with inviolable frontiers and to prevent aggression against UN members, there is an implied duty on governments to co-operate in effective arms trade regulation. And it must be in the interest of all states that these principles be defended. Article 2.5 of the UN Charter commits states to 'give the [UN] every assistance in any action it takes.' All UN member states are furthermore committed to 'refrain from giving assistance to any state against which the [UN] is taking preventive or enforcement action' and to 'establish standing mechanisms for the national regulation of their arms exports in order to be in a position to enforce mandatory arms embargoes' (Anthony [1991], p.1). Embargoes – such as the mandatory embargo imposed on South Africa in 1977 – are not the only issue, however. States must meet a variety of other obligations in international law, such as not supporting terrorist groups. Obligations of this nature again imply a duty on states and governments to have the means to supervise and control any transfer of arms, ammunition and military equipment, whatever the circumstances of the transaction (Blom-Cooper, p.100). International humanitarian law, otherwise known as the laws of war, can also require governments to co-operate in restricting the traffic of certain categories of weapons.

Ethics

Mention of the laws of war introduces the moral dimension to the discussion. Humanitarian law stigmatizes certain military practices and weapons as inhumane, indiscriminate or disproportionate. But it is not just the conduct of war which raises ethical objections and questions. As the recent campaign against anti-personnel land-mines illustrates, arguments from the humanitarian perspective can influence the discussion of defence-related trade. Anti-personnel land-mines have been distributed in their millions around the world in recent decades. But the problem is that unexploded mines – small and often undetectable to the naked eye or mine-detecting equipment – will lie dormant for many years and even decades, long after the war has passed into memory, until trodden on and activated by an innocent passer-by. As a result, thousands of deaths and injuries are caused every year in war-ravaged countries such as Cambodia and Afghanistan. Often the victims are children, and mine injuries can in any case have a desperate effect on subsistence farming communities. An international campaign against anti-personnel land-mines was begun in the early 1990s. One goal of the campaign was to ban the export of mines. Support for the campaign and for an export ban grew steadily, both in the United Nations and other international bodies, and in many national governments. But what is perhaps most striking about the land-mine campaign is its 'bottom-up' approach and its success in galvanizing public opinion on the issue. In this way, public disquiet about the ethics of making, using and exporting anti-personnel land-mines has had a direct and powerful influence upon governments and multilateral organizations, in some cases resulting in a radical redefinition of the national interest in order to take account of popular, humanitarian conviction.

Yet discussion of the ethics of selling arms can soon become rather entrenched. At one extreme lies the argument that weapons are morally neutral, that 'weapons do not make war, people do.' The bitter conflict over the separation of India and Pakistan in 1947 is often cited as evidence of destruction, killing and cruelty on a vast scale achieved without the benefit of modern weaponry. Events in Rwanda in 1994 provide a more recent illustration of the same argument. By this argument, moral concern about the transfer or possession of certain types of weapons is a misplaced, self-indulgent and at times also rather condescending obsession with technology; the only proper subject for examination should be the intention of the maker, owner or buyer of the weapon, and the moral quality of that intention. In any case, the argument might continue, it is difficult to define sustainable, objective moral criteria. Even important principles, such as the need to enable states to defend against aggression, or the need to deny arms to oppressive regimes, may in practice prove to be difficult to apply universally and beg many secondary questions which can only be answered in context. There is, for example, no universal agreement on what makes an appropriate or 'legitimate' level of self-defence, and a convincing definition of 'aggression' has so far eluded the United Nations legal experts. Defence-related trade, the argument might conclude, therefore takes place in a moral vacuum; there may be reasons why governments should intervene in the arms trade, but morality is not one of them.

At the other extreme of the ethical debate lies the proposition that defence-related trade is more causative than symptomatic of conflict and is therefore an ethical issue in its own right. Inter-war reaction against the 'merchants of death' who, allegedly, fuelled the 1914–18 war, illustrates this thinking, as does the currently popular analogy between defence-related trade and the illegal trade in narcotics, with talk of tackling the 'arms pushers' who corrupt and manipulate their 'victims'. The proposition extends into the notion that certain machines and technologies, far from being morally 'neutral', can be described as 'offensive' or 'destabilizing' and should therefore be banned or subject to special controls.

As the basis for informed, balanced thinking about defence-related trade, neither of these alternatives is especially helpful. The first approach begins to suggests that the international system is reducible to a ruthless, Darwinian free-for-all, in which the goal of policy is no more or less than the security and well-being of the state. The first approach might also be hinting, somewhat fatalistically, that officials and policy-makers are merely ciphers, trapped in what one writer has described as a "Greek tragedy, the tragedy of necessity, where the feeling aroused in the spectator is 'What a pity it had to be this way,'" (Stoessinger, p.80). Yet even the most convinced adherent to *realpolitik*, and the most determined patriot, must at some point be drawn into making some form of ethical judgement and choice, perhaps against his better judgement. National interest, by one definition, far from being the austere and amoral excuse for national self-gratification which might be supposed, is based upon the 'values of the national community, values which can be regarded as the product of its culture and as the expression of its sense of cohesion, values which define for men what they believe to be right or just' (Frankel, p.95). Another, related argument is that while it might be difficult to see international affairs being directed by considerations of *personal* morality, there is nevertheless a moral code of sorts, known as 'state morality'. In international affairs, politicians owe their first allegiance to their state; the collection of moral beings on whose behalf they act. This allegiance – responsibility or sense of duty – is the closest thing to a moral code in international affairs. Winston Churchill summed up the argument in plain language: 'The Sermon on the Mount is the last word in Christian ethics. Still, it is not on these terms that Ministers assume their responsibilities of guiding states.' And if politicians do indeed feel themselves caught up in a Greek tragedy, they should be aware that their electorate is unlikely to have much patience for their plight and will instead expect their representatives to make decisions for which they – and not destiny – will be held accountable.

Adherents to the second approach reject the idea that morality can somehow be divisible, preferring instead a direct and indissoluble connection between personal and international moral standards. Uncompromising faith in a divine ordering, or in the ultimate goodness of human nature, can offer either a spiritual or a secular route to pacifism, forgiveness and to the idea that mankind is being obstructed, by arms traders and even some machines, from achieving a natural state of global harmony. But all this seems out of place at a time when aggressors, dictators and other unsavoury characters plainly exist, and when more might be expected on the scene in future. And if such characters are in evidence, is it not prudent to be ready for self-defence by maintaining a well-equipped army; are the faithful not obliged to resist evil and tyranny, rather than submit to it?

The ethical debate on defence-related trade may be doomed to vacillate fruitlessly between these irreconcilable positions, and may as a result offer little in terms of concrete policy advice. What is more certain, however, is that democratic governments will face continuing pressure from vocal and articulate sections of the electorate motivated, at the very least, by a general, moral disquiet about the conduct and consequences of defence-related trade or by a more specific conviction; the campaign against anti-personnel land-mines could prove to have been a turning-point in the relationship between government export control policy-making and personal moral standards. For this reason, if for no other, it has now become impossible to exclude ethical considerations altogether from the arms trade debate. But how, and at what political level, ethical standards are framed, how they might be fed in to a policy-making machinery, and whether governments will take them seriously and if not at what cost, are all questions which will be debated for some time to come.

NATIONAL EXPORT CONTROL SYSTEMS

Turning to the form of national arms export controls, the first point to note is that most arms-exporting states have had ample experience of the possibilities and difficulties of supervising and regulating their participation in the international arms market. Several European governments, such as those of France, Italy and Britain, began to develop formal national export control systems during the 1930s. The United States also has a long tradition of export controls, dating back to the 1949 Export Control Act. The 1949 Act, passed in the context of rapidly deteriorating East-West relations, gave the executive branch of the US government 'broad authority' in creating, administering and enforcing the export control system, an authority which was 'largely exempt from the usual process of public comment and virtually immune from judicial review' (Wallerstein and Snyder, p.310). The concept of national control, and with it the culture of secrecy which has often obscured debate of the arms trade, were therefore well established by the time the Cold War began in earnest in the 1950s. Driven by the Cold War confrontation, governments in North America, Western Europe and elsewhere introduced increasingly elaborate export control systems which often shared certain features, among them the following:

•A list of weapons and goods, the export of which required a special licence;

•A list of 'target' countries, either proscribed or preferred;

•A list of criteria or standards against which applications to export might be judged;

•A licence application procedure and a bureaucracy to enable inter-departmental consultation;

•A method by which licence grants and denials could be verified and policed nationally, a customs service at frontiers and ports, and a set of penalties with the means to impose them;
•A method to guarantee the 'end-use', or non re-export of the licensed and exported consignment to a destination which would otherwise not have been licensed.

There were, however, important differences across the range of national systems, reflecting different legal and constitutional practices and foreign policy expectations. The pursuit of rigorous national export control policies was sometimes more declaratory than real, particularly among governments which also promoted arms exports through special governmental offices and provided soft loans and export credit guarantees to help weapons exporters. These differences in the scope and quality of national export controls became more and more entrenched as the years passed; in 1991 the European Commission carried out a survey of national export control systems throughout the EC and discovered that, more than four decades after the supposed renaissance of Western European export controls, systems were far from uniform and in some cases standards were extremely low (Mueller, p.11). In some cases, national controls have been simply inadequate to the task, usually where customs procedures and the policing of ports have been concerned. In other cases, the system has been framed in such a way as to leave the government concerned with the maximum flexibility and the minimum of binding, legislative commitment. The current policy of the British government, for example, is to judge export applications 'on a case by case basis in the light of established criteria' (House of Commons, para. 26). Some countries, such as Sweden and Austria, have very rigorous export control systems, while others prefer the more pragmatic British approach; in late 1994, the Federal Republic of Germany, often cited as having one of the most restrictive approaches to arms exports among Western European states, relaxed its rules for weapons exports in order to 'fall in line with emerging European standards for arms exports', standards which the German government perceived to be more elastic than those which had been imposed nationally.[1]

Matrix Churchill and the Scott Inquiry

Britain, one of the major Western arms exporters, has recently been host to a comprehensive critique of arms and technology export control practices after the Cold War. Early in 1990 it was revealed that British engineering firms were heavily involved in Iraqi plans to acquire massive cannons – the so-called Supergun Affair – and other military manufacturing equipment. In October 1990 executives of one firm – Matrix Churchill – were arrested for supplying machine tools to Iraq, allegedly in contravention of export regulations. Following Iraq's defeat by US–led coalition forces in the Gulf War of 1990–91, and the discovery that Western European firms had been important accessories – unwittingly or otherwise – to Saddam Hussein's military procurement programme, public and media pressure mounted for the 'gun-runners' to be exposed and punished.

The trial of Matrix Churchill executives opened and collapsed in November 1992, as a result of inadequacies and contradictions in the prosecution. The British government's response to the fiasco was to initiate a judicial inquiry into the case. The inquiry – under Lord Justice Richard Scott – opened in May 1993. After almost 3 years of investigation and many postponements, the inquiry reached its conclusion with the publication of the 2,300-page Scott Report in February 1996.[2] The issue at the centre of the inquiry was the nature of government export control guidelines regarding the export of 'lethal equipment' and/or 'defence equipment' to Iran and Iraq during the Gulf War of the 1980s. Had the guidelines been modified at any point? Had Parliament been informed of any modifications? Or had Parliament deliberately been misled by government ministers? In time, the report may prove to have been a milestone in British constitutional history but it is as yet too early to gauge its significance. The report does, however, contain some more concrete recommendations concerning Britain's export control system. For example, the report criticizes the reliance of successive British governments on emergency powers dating back to 1939, and calls for a modern export control system more appropriate for the post-Cold War world. The report calls for more openness and Parliamentary oversight, and argues that the foreign policy dimensions of export controls should be openly discussed. Finally, the report asks whether it is right that technologically developed countries should use export control systems to maintain a 'technology gap' between themselves and less-developed countries.

The most charitable summary of the Scott Report's findings would be that they provide a valuable indication of the complexity of national export control systems, and a demonstration of the conflicting demands upon policy-makers. But one important lesson of the whole inquiry process is that the export of dual-use, civil/military technology and manufacturing equipment can be just as significant in strategic and geopolitical terms as the transfer of complete weapons systems. Yet it is extremely difficult to find clear, lasting and functional definitions of these commodities. Speaking of business deals with the Soviet Union, Paul Henderson, one of the Matrix Churchill executives, summarized the dual-use problem in his autobiography:

While it was unusual for us not to know where the machines were being installed in the Soviet Union, there was nothing extraordinary about using machine tools for military purposes. Some of our biggest customers had always been munitions and armaments factories. One of the key features of machine tools is versatility. A lathe or milling machine can be configured to produce parts for a car or a military personnel carrier, parts for a domestic appliance or for a rifle. Even if we had supervised the installation of the machines and set them up to manufacture civilian components in the Soviet Union, any competent engineer could have made the adjustments necessary to turn out military products.[3]

THE RATIONALE FOR INTERNATIONAL CO-ORDINATION

It is clear that, for a variety of pragmatic, legal and moral reasons, governments on the supply side of defence-related trade are motivated or pressurized at least to manage their involvement in the market. All states involved in the trade have developed some sort of management system, and it is at this unilateral level that most management of defence-related trade has taken place. Some analysts argue that the trend towards multilateralism is misplaced, and that efforts at the unilateral level offer the only real possibility of control (Laurance [1993], pp.176–9). But there are good reasons for states to co-operate in arms trade regulation and to join like-minded countries in a more or less structured, multilateral arms export management arrangement. In the second half of the twentieth century the most obvious structure was the Cold War itself, with industries and governments on each side of the divide generally having to respect the bipolar ordering of global politics and strategy. Loyalties often changed during the Cold War, with some countries becoming adept at 'shopping around' for their weapons and military equipment, effectively ignoring the niceties of the confrontation between the Western Alliance and the Soviet Union. But with the end of the Cold War 'shopping around' has become the norm, rather than the exception. Without Cold War 'spheres of influence', there seems to be no alternative source of market discipline. The growing diversity of the global market, the spread of manufacturing capability, and the early stages of the internationalization of defence industry demand a more sophisticated form of multilateral management. Increasingly therefore, governments have been drawn – or pressurised – into co-operative initiatives to manage defence-related trade, albeit not entirely successfully.

Co-operative Export Control – the Options

When governments decide, for whatever reason, that the management of defence-related trade can best be achieved co-operatively, a number of options present themselves. The simplest conceivable form of export control co-operation is that which takes place on an *ad hoc* basis, as circumstances require, and which results in jointly implemented arms or technology embargoes. With no attempt to organize the co-operation in any formal or institutional way, and no attempt to justify the co-operation through an appeal to a higher political or moral authority, initiatives of this sort might best be described as reactive, concerted, militant diplomacy. Such agreements, made at short notice and for a short period, might be relatively easy to make and could have a rapid effect, both on domestic public opinion and on the 'target' state. But *ad hoc* initiatives involving just a few like-minded states might also prove easy for the participants to leave, and equally easy for the targets to evade. Governments are accordingly persuaded both that co-operation should have some form of organization, and that the initiative should include as many of the relevant sellers and buyers as possible or appropriate. Another consideration could be that governments which appear too willing to implement unilateral, *ad hoc* embargoes might become known in the market-place as politically and commercially unreliable. The merchant's reputation for trustworthiness and dependability will be a prized asset in all areas of industry and commerce. This is particularly the case where 'buyer's market' conditions prevail and the thwarted client can simply take his business elsewhere, and especially so when arms and technology are being traded and governments and societies might consider their very survival to be at stake. In these circumstances, supplier governments might wish to legitimize any controversial action they choose to take by, say, a UN Security Council Resolution or by appealing to principles such as the advancement of human rights, liberal democracy or free market economics. Another consideration, which must militate against the rapid imposition and relaxation of *ad hoc* embargoes, is that with a weapons research, development and training 'package' often lasting well over a decade, governments and industry are likely to resist being labelled by potential clients as fickle and easily swayed by calls for an embargo.

Effective co-operation in the management of defence-related trade by the supplying states therefore suggests three prerequisites. First, the initiative will seek to be organized and institutionalized, rather than appear merely a casual arrangement between governments. Second, the participants will draw upon a higher authority rather than appear to be driven by mere *realpolitik* and national interest. Legal and political authority might come from the United Nations, while moral authority might come from religious conviction or from some other set of principles. Finally, the initiative is likely to take place over time rather than appear spontaneous and short-lived.

Co-operation in the control of defence-related trade might take one of two forms. The key to the first, which might be called a 'coercive trade-management regime', is that the goal is agreed by the sellers but not accepted by the buyers, or 'targets'. There are two variants of this type of initiative. The first is a relatively straightforward matter of denial and domination, the best example of which would be the conditions imposed on a defeated state. Rather more subtle, and much more complex, enforcement can also be a matter of drawn-out, systematic trade restrictions such as the CoCom initiative of 1949–94 and, more recently, the various WMD technology-transfer control regimes such as the Nuclear Suppliers Group and the Missile Technology Control Regime. By this more systematic model, clients might be required to accept certain conditions regarding their overall military expenditure, their relations with neighbouring states, their support for arms control initiatives and even the character of their society and government in exchange for access to the market for weapons and defence-related technology.

The second broad approach is to seek what might be termed a 'mutual regime', one which is genuinely multilateral, involving sellers from all round the world as well as buyers, and which is based upon a universal – or at least widely held – set of norms and values. The difficulty of identifying these shared norms and standards among the world's arms suppliers – fiercely competitive for market share and often with very different cultural inheritances – by which to regulate the international arms market, will be discussed more fully in the next chapter. The various initiatives to prevent the proliferation of nuclear, biological and chemical weapons of mass destruction could provide some sort of a model, although there are features of these regimes (such as the export control arrangements) which might appear to have more in common with supply-side denial rather than mutual agreement. The presumption against 'horizontal' proliferation of weapons of mass destruction (rather than 'vertical' proliferation, by which the protagonists simply increased and improved their strategic arsenals) largely transcended the Cold War confrontation and still has a considerable international constituency. Complacency in this regard may, however, be increasingly misplaced. Since the end of the Cold War there have been several instances of acquisition and even use of WMD in obvious contravention of the various regimes. Maverick WMD research and development programmes are hardly a new phenomenon and to some extent serve to emphasize the general non-proliferation norm.

What would prove far more hazardous is the erosion of this general norm among more responsible states and governments. The difficulties in negotiating the review and extension of the Nuclear Non-Proliferation Treaty and the unhurried ratification of the Chemical Weapons Convention may indicate an unwelcome erosion of faith in the blanket presumption against WMD proliferation. However vulnerable the WMD non-proliferation regimes are becoming, they are still considerably more solid and durable than anything which might be described as a norm against conventional proliferation. It is not a straightforward matter to transfer WMD non-proliferation ideas and practices to the conventional area; while there are 'unambiguous ethical, pragmatic and power-political' reasons to prevent nuclear proliferation, and 'considerable international acceptance' of those reasons, 'In the area of conventional arms there are no such unambiguous answers' (Simpson, p. 237).

MULTILATERAL EXPORT CONTROL SYSTEMS

There are plenty of reasons why states should wish to collaborate in regulating the arms trade. Although there are grounds to be sceptical as to the outcome of such collaboration, what are the mechanisms which are currently available to states? This section looks at the main initiatives, launched since the end of the Cold War, to achieve supervision and/or regulation of the international arms market.

The Gulf War and After

As indicated in the introductory chapter, the end of the Cold War and the Iraq/Kuwait crisis in 1990–1991 were followed by a series of declarations and initiatives. The results have been mixed. The Group of Seven leading industrialized democracies (G7), for example, published their 'Declaration on Conventional Arms Transfers and NBC [nuclear, biological and chemical] Non-Proliferation' at their annual economic summit in London in July 1991. The G7 were especially concerned with the accretion of 'disproportionate arsenals' of weapons and military equipment and called for transparency, consultation, common guidelines and action to prevent further 'destabilizing' arms transfers. The G7 declaration also addressed, albeit briefly, the relationship between military expenditure and 'sound economic policy' in developing countries. The G7 initiative never translated into a formal programme or management system; the most charitable epitaph on the declaration would be that it laid down certain criteria and objectives which individual G7 governments pursued elsewhere. More hope was held for the initiative launched in October 1991 by the Permanent Five members of the UN Security Council (the 'P5' – the United States, the then Soviet Union, the People's Republic of China, Great Britain and France). At their meeting in London, the P5 agreed to set any arms export decisions against mutually acceptable 'Guidelines for Conventional Arms Transfers', promised to 'exchange information for the purpose of meaningful consultation,' and agreed to meet at regular intervals. Negotiations were never friction-free. The main sticking point was whether partners should expect some sort of oversight over the planned exports of other participants, or whether the information should be retrospective summaries of weapons delivered. Disagreement also emerged over the geographical scope of the process, particularly whether it should be global or confined to the Middle East. Another difficulty lay in comparing weapon types; how, for example, could a fair distinction be made between a medium-sized ballistic missile armed with a conventional warhead, and a long-range bomber or ground attack aircraft? The initiative was, in any case, short-lived and lasted, fitfully, only until October 1992 when the PRC withdrew, in protest at the US sale of F-16 fighter aircraft to Taiwan. France subsequently sold Mirage fighters to Taiwan and once again invoked the ire of the mainland Chinese government. It is unlikely that the initiative will ever be revived, although it is possible that some of the less ambitious goals of the P5 process could be met in the successor to CoCom, the so-called Wassenaar Arrangement, discussed below.

Another initiative, which has lasted longer but has as yet had little concrete impact, was that launched by the Conference on Security and Co-operation in Europe (CSCE).[4] Following declarations made in June 1991 and January 1992, the CSCE published their 'Principles and Guidelines Governing Conventional Arms Transfers' in November 1993. Unlike the P5 initiative, the CSCE document included a 'human rights criterion', an addition which caused some difficulty for negotiators during summer 1993. The CSCE guidelines, reflecting in large part ideas already proposed in the P5 initiative and in the European Community, were presented as 'recommendations' to member states but were not binding in any way.

If the G7, P5 and CSCE initiatives have had disappointing results, there might be more room for optimism regarding three other post–Cold War arms trade management initiatives; the UN Register of Conventional Arms, the 'Wassenaar Arrangement' in succession to CoCom, and the European Union arms and technology export control initiatives. Even in these cases, however, the prospects are not boundless.

The UN Conventional Arms Register
In July 1991 the United Nations published a document entitled *Study on Ways and Means of Promoting Transparency in International Transfers of Conventional Arms*. Later that year at the UN, a draft resolution jointly sponsored by the EC and Japan was put before the General Assembly. On 9 December 1991, passed by 150 votes to none against with two abstentions (Cuba and Iraq), the draft became A/46/36/L – *Transparency in Armaments*. This resolution called upon the UN Secretary-General to establish a *universal and non-discriminatory register of conventional arms, to include international arms transfers*. As a result of last-minute amendments to the draft resolution, in the end registration was to be of conventional arms generally, rather than just their transfer. This small amendment points to a central feature of the continuing debate on the value of the Register and its future. One of the main reasons for the failure of earlier attempts in the twentieth century to account for the transfer of weapons was that the result would have been *discriminatory* – revealing the behaviour of those countries reliant upon imports of weapons while ignoring those which were able to procure weapons domestically. The final version of the resolution established a Register which would primarily record and reveal

transfers of weapons, but which would also, in time, present information on domestic procurement and existing holdings. States were 'called upon' to provide data on imports and exports of certain categories of conventional weapons by 30 April each year, and were 'invited' to provide information in various other categories, including procurement and holdings.

The resolution also called for a panel of experts to work on detailed implementation issues. The panel reported in August 1992. The bulk of the panel's effort was in agreeing on what categories of weapon should be covered by the Register and in what format national reports should be made. A second UN Group of Experts discussed the operation and further development of the Register, reporting to the Secretary-General in summer 1994. Discussions and negotiations continue, but since spring 1993, the deadline for returns covering the calendar year 1992, states have been providing data on annual exports and imports of weapons in the following categories; tanks, armoured combat vehicles, large calibre artillery systems, combat aircraft (fixed wing), attack helicopters, warships, and missiles and missile launchers. Participation in the Register has been steady at roughly 50 per cent of the membership of the UN; 92 countries provided returns for the first year of operation (1992), 89 countries for 1993, and 93 countries for 1994.

The Register is the 'only agreed global initiative designed to address the problem of accumulations and transfers of conventional arms' (Chalmers and Greene, p.4) The key feature of the Register is that participation is entirely voluntary; the Register has no legal status and no enforcement mechanism. This may explain why about half of the UN's membership have ignored the initiative. But it was precisely this absence of supervision and direction which, it was hoped, would encourage states to participate. And most of the world's main exporters and importers of arms do indeed participate, ensuring that, in one form or another, the vast majority of transactions are covered. Although not a control mechanism as such, and although no attempt is made in the Register or by the UN to decide which transfers are acceptable and which are not, the Register could nevertheless provide a foundation for subsequent arms control agreements, or for confidence-building on a regional basis. The Register has many critics, and even its keenest supporters are not starry-eyed about its potential. Apart from the level of participation, critics point to the lack of any means of verification, the lack of any ceilings for arms acquisitions, the restricted scope of the Register, particularly as regards the absence of small arms (rifles, small mortars, land-mines etc.) from the list of weapons. Other than helping to expose certain transactions, the Register also makes no direct attempt to deal with the illegal arms trade.

The key to the future of the Register, and the issue which is most likely to determine the level of participation, is the question of placing holdings and domestic procurement of conventional weapons on an equal footing with exports and imports. Until this is achieved, the Register is likely to be viewed by those states which rely on arms imports as a discriminatory initiative and it is therefore unlikely to achieve even its limited potential. The expansion of the Register to include holdings and procurement has been deferred until at least 1997, when another Group of Governmental Experts will assemble to review the initiative (Chalmers and Greene, p.10).

From CoCom to the 'Wassenaar Arrangement'

The first post-war attempt at multilateral export control was the Co-ordinating Committee for Multilateral Export Controls (CoCom), founded in 1949 as the uneasy diplomacy of the post-war years was developing rapidly into the entrenched hostility of the Cold War. CoCom was never a formal, treaty-based arrangement, and its proceedings were not held in the public eye. The organization was based in the US Embassy in Paris, where regular meetings took place and where a permanent Co-ordinating Group carried out its work.

Sometimes described as the 'economic arm of NATO', CoCom's aim was to restrict the supply of key technology and commodities to Cold War adversaries. The Soviet Union and its satellites, China and other countries all appeared on a 'Country List' of proscribed destinations. The CoCom partners (NATO members less Iceland, plus Japan and, since 1989, Australia), agreed to national enforcement of agreed controls on goods and technologies contained in three commodity lists which were updated every four years. The International Munitions List (IML), covered conventional arms, munitions and items which were unequivocally military. The International Atomic Energy List (IAEL) dealt with technology needed for nuclear weapons design and testing. Finally, the International Industrial List (IIL) included items with dual civil/military use. The IIL covered a huge range of products and technology, from carbon fibre to silicon-based micro-circuitry. For its participants, the importance of CoCom can hardly be overstated; by one account CoCom was nothing less than 'the principal forum for the Western allies to agree upon and implement restrictions on trade in weapons and dual-use goods and technologies with Soviet-bloc and other Communist countries' (American Bar Association, p.3). National export controls were heavily influenced by CoCom, and the European Union dual-use regulation – discussed below – developed in its shadow.

CoCom was both a tool of economic warfare and a general strategic embargo. It was always a difficult matter of good intelligence and sound judgement to know which goods and technologies contributed to Soviet military capability, and which Western industries should accordingly suffer restrictions. It was generally accepted that the most CoCom could achieve was to delay the acquisition of leading technologies by the communist bloc, thereby ensuring that the West maintained the technological upper hand. But, in spite of the perceived presence of an overwhelming, unifying military threat to the West, CoCom was never free of controversy and misunderstanding among its partners. Having agreed unanimously on the content of the destination and commodity lists and any amendments, CoCom partners had to seek a 'general exception' if they wished to export a listed good to a proscribed destination. Since an exception could also only be agreed unanimously, each partner effectively had a 'right to veto the sales of others' (Roberts, p.165). However, since CoCom was a voluntary organization without a treaty base, the use of the veto always had to be set against the risk that the offended partner could simply withdraw from the scheme. Some partners made use of 'administrative exception notes' by which they stated that certain items would be subjected to national control alone, and would not be made subject to collective review in CoCom and therefore vulnerable to a veto.

Although the end of the Cold War brought the rationale for CoCom into question, many continued to argue for a multilateral forum to control the export of sensitive technologies. Partly in response to the expansion of WMD non-proliferation regimes into the dual-use area, and partly to present a more accommodating face to the technology-starved former Soviet Union and its allies, in 1990 CoCom began to reduce its IIL to a 'Core List' of especially sensitive technology. This list was finalized in February 1992, although disagreements remained over controls on certain technologies such as computers and telecommunications. May 1992 saw the creation of an informal CoCom Co-operation Forum (CCF). The CCF was an acknowledgement that many former Warsaw Treaty states needed Western technology for their economic stability, and that several of these states could now be removed from CoCom's Country List (as was, for example, Hungary in February 1992). Furthermore, the perception was gaining ground that the acquisition of weapons of mass destruction by certain Third World countries, and even terrorist organizations, was a far greater danger and one which would require effective, broad co-operation. So the idea was born of using CoCom as a general export control mechanism, rather than a more focused, East-West technology embargo or weapon of economic warfare.

At a meeting of CoCom partners at The Hague on 16 November 1993 it was agreed that the scheme was now defunct, and that CoCom controls would be phased out by 31 March 1994. On the eve of the organization's demise, however, the partners agreed that a replacement body should be in place by the end of 1994. For the interim period, partners agreed to maintain the commodity lists – the 'Core List' residue of the IIL now became known as the 'Interim List' – while accepting more flexibility and national discretion in the granting of export licences. CoCom was duly wound up on 31 March 1994, while negotiations continued to find an appropriate successor regime. The question of the membership of any new body provoked controversy. Those who saw in the new body a means to manage global dual-use technology and conventional weapons transfers argued that Russia must be made a member of any new organization from the outset, with China and other states also joining eventually. Britain and France, in particular, argued that the new body would have little meaning without Russian membership. But Russia's arms sales to Iran became a sticking point, particularly for the United States. Russia's pledge in September 1994 that it would halt future arms sales to Iran ignored existing contracts to supply advanced weapon systems, and generally failed to convince US critics. It was not until June 1995 that Russia and the United States finally reached agreement. The last of the five sessions of talks concerning the replacement for CoCom thus began in September 1995 between the original seventeen partners, the six 'co-operating partners' (Austria, Finland, Ireland, New Zealand, Sweden and Switzerland), and a group of former CoCom 'Country List' states (Russia, Poland, Hungary, the Czech Republic and Slovakia).

Procedural disputes had dogged earlier discussion of CoCom's successor, but during the autumn 1995 negotiations in The Hague, the question of membership ceased to be a significant obstruction. Negotiators were also determined that, whatever the outcome of their deliberations, *something* would have to be in place by the early months of 1996. Discussion therefore moved rapidly to more important substantive issues. The outcome was the Wassenaar Arrangement on Export Controls for Conventional Arms and Dual-Use Goods and Technologies, named after the town outside The Hague where all five rounds of the 'post-CoCom' negotiations had been held. The new regime was announced in a very brief formal declaration made on behalf of the 28 participating countries on 19 December 1995, while a much longer, confidential document of several hundred pages was passed to governments for further analysis. The six-sentence declaration indicated that 'initial elements of the new arrangement' had been agreed, that a Preparatory Committee would begin working to develop the arrangement in January 1996, and that the first plenary meeting of the new scheme would take place in early April 1996 in Vienna, where the regime and its small secretariat would henceforth be based. But for the details – such as they were – of what had been agreed, many analysts looked to the text of a speech made in January 1996 by a senior US State Department official.

One important feature of the new arrangement is, apparently, that it will seek to establish scrutiny over the exports, not only of conventional arms, but also of weapons manufacturing technologies and key 'dual-use' technologies and components which can have both military and civilian uses. With this in mind, delegates at Wassenaar accepted, in principle, that the backbone of the arrangement should be two commodity lists. The first list would deal with weapons and would correspond fairly closely to the weapon types listed in both the November 1990 Conventional Armed Forces in Europe Treaty and the UN Register. The second list would cover dual-use goods and technologies: perhaps as many as 100 different items such as machine tools, computers and communications equipment in three lists – 'basic', 'sensitive', and 'very sensitive'. But final agreement was still needed as to the precise composition of the two lists and how they would be updated and amended. Rather less agreement was reached where the 'target' of the regime was concerned. Delegates apparently accepted the US argument that the activities of the new body should at the very least be focused upon the arms and technology acquisition plans of four so-called pariah states: Iran, Iraq, Libya and North Korea. But there was much less acceptance of another US idea to focus the arrangement on particularly unstable or tense regions of the world; this sort of thinking, with respect to the Middle East, had prompted the US initiative which led to the ill-fated 'P5' scheme discussed above. The United States had also been keen on prior notification of arms transfers. The Wassenaar Arrangement may be a loose, consensual scheme without a CoCom-style veto system, but the American view was that prior notification would at least allow other members of the arrangement at least to voice a protest at the planned sale. Yet this idea had gone down particularly badly with Western European participants, especially France and the United Kingdom, whose defence industrial sector was perceived to be rather more vulnerable than that in the United States and therefore in need of as much protection as possible from external competition and undercutting. The United States hoped to secure agreement on prior notification in the so-called small group on arms. But this group – made up of the six largest weapons exporters (the United States, France, the United Kingdom, Russia, Italy and Germany) and organized as an informal arrangement-within-an-arrangement – not only failed to agree on prior notification, but also raised questions about the purpose of the Wassenaar Arrangement as a whole.

With so much disagreement remaining on key substantive issues, it is clear that a great deal more work will be needed to make the Wassenaar Arrangement useful and respected. The scheme may at present have wider participation than CoCom, but without much closer agreement on the character, procedures and scope of the initiative it is unlikely to be as rigorous or effective. At present, the broad aims and style of the Wassenaar Arrangement are closer to the transparency approach adopted by the UN Register than to the embargo/denial approach embodied by CoCom, and it remains to be seen whether states will find this awkwardly-titled venture a valuable addition to their wardrobe of multilateral commitments. The omens are not good; the first plenary session of the Wassenaar Arrangement in Vienna in early April 1996 ended unsuccessfully, following deep disagreements between the United States and Russia. Russia refused to disclose details of its arms sales around the world and was concerned about the attempt by the Arrangement to stigmatize certain 'pariah' countries, several of which are important consumers of Russian military products. Further negotiations were scheduled to take place in July 1996.

European Union Initiatives

Finally, mention should be made of two attempts by the European Community/Union (EC/EU) and its member states to supervise and/or regulate the export of both conventional weapons and defence-related technology. The Gulf War of 1990–91 had important repercussions for several members of the European Community; some of Iraq's major arms suppliers had been EC members, and in some cases European troops in the US-led coalition faced Iraqis wielding high-specification weaponry which had been exported from Europe. After the war, as the United Nations organized a series of inspections of Iraqi weapons research and manufacturing facilities, it also became clear that several EC states had supplied, knowingly or otherwise, weapons-related technology to Iraq. In some cases, this technology had assisted in the development and production of weapons of mass destruction and in the construction of the bizarre, very long range 'supergun' which was to have fired massive shells at Israel. On a more general level, the handling of the Iraq/Kuwait crisis was portrayed in some quarters as proof of the inadequacy of EC foreign policy co-operation in the more loosely ordered post-Cold War world. This perception contributed to the review of EC foreign and security policy-making which had been set in motion in December 1990 at the Inter-Governmental Conference on Political Union, the conference which culminated in the 1991 Maastricht Treaty. With Europe's defence industries increasingly reliant on weapons exports, with some sense of responsibility for having allowed Saddam Hussein to build up a 'destabilizing and excessive' collection of weapons and technology, and with calls to review and tighten foreign and security policy co-operation, the debate in Western Europe developed rapidly, with pressure mounting on governments and the European Commission alike to improve and co-ordinate their export control systems. As far as arms exports were concerned, the first step was taken in June 1991 with the publication of seven 'criteria' by which EC members would gauge their arms export decisions. One more criterion was added twelve months later. The eight criteria read as follows:

The European Union Arms Export Criteria

1. Respect for the international commitments of the member states of the Community, in particular the sanctions decreed by the Security Council of the United Nations and those decreed by the Community, and agreements on non-proliferation and other subjects, as well as other international obligations;

2. The respect of human rights in the country of final destination;

3. The internal situation in the country of final destination, as a function of the existence of tensions or internal armed conflicts;

4. The preservation of regional peace, security and stability;

5. The national security of the member states and of territories whose external relations are the responsibility of a member state, as well as that of friendly and allied countries;

6. The behaviour of the buyer country with regard to the international community, as regards in particular its attitude to terrorism, the nature of its alliances, and respect for international law;

7. The existence of a risk that the equipment will be diverted within the buyer country or re-exported under undesirable conditions.

8. [Added in June 1992] The compatibility of the arms exports with the technical and economic capacity of the recipient country, taking into account the desirability that States should achieve their legitimate needs of security and defence with the least diversion for armaments of human and economic resources.

Several governments stressed at the time, and have done so repeatedly since, that the criteria were not the first step towards a *common policy* on arms exports and need not be applied at all times and in all cases. Governments also developed a Common Reference List of weapons and other military equipment, a graduated 'menu of options' offering four levels of military embargoes, and sought to harmonise national bureaucratic procedures. But once again, much stress was laid upon the fact that these measures amounted to the harmonization of the different policies of member states, rather than the creation of a single, central policy. At the heart of the matter was the clash between two very different approaches to co-operation and policy-making within the European Community/Union. On one hand, there was the supranational style of co-operation where the European Commission had 'competence', as in industrial, commercial and agricultural policies. On the other hand, there were those areas of policy, such as foreign affairs, defence and domestic judicial systems, where many governments saw their 'national prerogative' to be irreducible and argued that co-operation and policy-making would have to be *inter-governmental*.   Where defence-related trade was concerned, the symbol of the clash of approaches lay in Article 223 of the 1958 Treaty of Rome establishing the European Economic Community. Article 223 reads as follows:

> *Article 223 of the Treaty of Rome*
> 1. The provisions of this Treaty shall not preclude the application of the following rules:
> a) No Member State shall be obliged to supply information the disclosure of which it considers contrary to the essential interests of its security;
> b) Any Member State may take such measures as it considers necessary for the protection of the essential interests of its security which are connected with the production of or trade in arms, munitions and war material; such measures shall not adversely affect the conditions of

competition in the common market regarding products which are not intended for specifically military purposes.

2. During the first year after the entry into force of this Treaty, the Council shall, acting unanimously, draw up a list of products to which the provisions of paragraph 1(b) shall apply.

3. The Council may, acting unanimously on a proposal from the Commission, make changes in this list.

Several attempts have been made to remove Article 223 from the Treaty, but it remains in force and continues to shape the way arms exports are viewed in the European Union. The fate of Article 223 is likely to be the subject of intense debate during the Turin Inter-Governmental Conference which began in March 1996 and is expected to last between 18 months and two years.

The European Union Dual-Use Export Control Regulation

It was soon realized, however, that under the complex rules laid down by the EEC Treaty and the Single European Act of 1986, Article 223 could not exclude supranational, European Commission involvement in some key aspects of defence-related trade, most significantly the export of 'dual-use' technology which could have both military and civil uses. If a commodity or technology could be shown to have a civil use, then movement of that item within the European Community, and its export to third parties, would both come under the more centralized rules of the Single European Market managed by the European Commission. Furthermore, governments would not be allowed to cite the military application of the technology as a means to 'derogate' from the rules of the Single Market and follow national practices. The result was that, distinct from the inter-governmental (and non-binding) arms export control 'criteria', an entirely different approach had to be taken to the multilateral control of exports of defence-related technology from the European Union. After several years of complex, drawn-out negotiations, on 1 July 1995 the European Union dual-use technology export control regulation came into force. The regulation is elaborate and ambitious, and stands as one of the most comprehensive attempts to tackle the problems of sensitive technology exports by any group of states. The regulation is also something of a novelty in that it has elements of both inter-governmental and supranational co-operation and decision-making. Some European Union governments argued that, however persuasive the case for expanding Single Market-style regulations into the area of defence-related technology, there were still some aspects of the trade which would have more to do with national defence, security and foreign policies than with the Common Commercial Policy and industrial integration. The outcome is in many respects an uneasy compromise; the European Commission has an important role in maintaining and overseeing the regulation and its legal and procedural bases, while governments have reserved for their own, less formal style of co-operation some of the more important, substantive aspects of decision-making.

CONCLUSION

There are many reasons why states should wish to control the international market in conventional weapons and related technology. Export control systems have been established at the national level in all major weapons and technology exporting states. These controls are, in the first place, designed to answer national requirements and preferences, but they also provide the foundation for collaboration with other, like-minded states. The received wisdom has it that effective regulation of the international arms market requires collaboration between both suppliers and recipients. Yet there seems to be all too little common ground between buyers and sellers. What is more – or perhaps as a consequence – the main sellers themselves have so far proved unable or unwilling to establish a viable regulatory system. Some explanations for this situation are offered in the next chapter.

NOTES

1. 'Germany Eases Rules for Weapons Exports', *Defense News*, 12 December 1994.

2. *Report of the Inquiry into the Export of Defence Equipment and Dual-Use Goods to Iraq and Related Prosecutions* (London:HMSO, February 1996).

3. P. Henderson, *The Unlikely Spy* (London: Bloomsbury, 1993), p.9.

4. Now known as the *Organisation* for Security and Co-operation in Europe (OSCE).

4

VISIONS AND VALUES

INTRODUCTION

It is often argued that the most effective arms trade management regime would be one which included all (or most) suppliers and recipients, obeying common standards and working towards common goals. Common sense suggests that this must be the case; to impose strict rules on just a few participants in a global market would be an invitation to competitors. But, for at least two reasons, this ideal condition seems unlikely to be achieved. The first problem reflects the practical difficulty of getting any large group of people or agencies to agree on anything, and there are almost 190 states members of the United Nations. Given the especially parochial character of international politics at present, the goal of a world-wide (or even near-world-wide) consensus on the question of the international arms market and its regulation – a level of agreement which could be convincing, could extend beyond the contingent interests of one or another group of states and which could underpin an international regime – might take some years to realize. Parochialism is being eroded, particularly by the global telecommunications 'revolution', but this erosion is a slow process and may in the end reveal an irreducible hard core of local loyalties and interests; even 'citizens of the world' live in a street or a village. The second difficulty is that when the search for consensus is examined closely (or 'deconstructed'), it appears to many observers – Western and non-Western alike – that the quest itself is only adding to the problem. Underlying much of the thinking about how to regulate international trade in strategic goods is a series of assumptions – often Western in origin – about the international order and about the 'suitability' of certain individuals, states, cultures and practices. But these assumptions are not necessarily shared by many states in the 'South', 'East' or 'developing world' which often see themselves, not so much as having been *participants* in, as *victims* of, the Cold War and Western ideological and strategic hegemony, and which now feel that their cultural and national interests are not best served by following dutifully a Western agenda. Ironically, therefore, while the search for consensus can seem to be a particularly urgent requirement for effective management of the arms trade, the search itself can result in still deeper divisions.

Since the end of the Cold War, there have been many attempts – largely by countries which manufacture and supply arms and which had been part of the Western camp during the Cold War – to establish multilateral agreements to restrain the export of conventional weapons and related technology. By mid–1996, however, these schemes had generally failed to meet the high standards which had initially been called for by the United Nations, by some governments, by vocal and determined campaigners and by sections of the media, all anxious that steps should be taken to prevent another destabilizing acquisition of weapons on the Iraqi model. Reactive, *ad hoc*, punitive arms embargoes – even those which contain an element of self-denial – do not present many difficulties for governments, either acting unilaterally or in concert. But a longer-term programme of self-discipline and self-denial can present awkward political and commercial challenges, and it has evidently proven difficult for arms-supplier states to move beyond the level of *ad hoc* embargoes to develop a more comprehensive and anticipatory approach to export controls. The need to support the domestic defence industry, technological diffusion, the spread of competitive arms manufacturing capacity and the lack of political and economic cohesion among suppliers, all go some way to explaining this situation. But this chapter suggests that there could also be more fundamental weaknesses in the idea of multilateral arms trade management.

DISAGREEING TO AGREE

Governments are pushed, for a variety of reasons, towards some form of multilateral regulation of the arms trade. Yet this impulse has so far had very limited effect. The complex task of balancing commercial, political and moral considerations would doubtless be made more easy by the identification of a principle or code by which to shape difficult decisions nationally and multilaterally. But it may equally be that no such value exists or could ever be identified, or that the norm being sought is no less than one which could deal with aggression, conflict and war itself. In any case, the search for such a code has so far been of more interest to analysts of the international arms trade than to participants in it. These same analysts, however, tend to agree on the difficulty of establishing and maintaining a set of general norms or values which might govern the transfer of conventional weapons and related technology. This is in part attributable to the character of the post-Cold War arms market, which emphasizes a competitive, non co-operative commercial logic and which makes it difficult even for like-minded suppliers to define common goals and rules by which to regulate their participation in the arms trade. Some hope has been expressed that the United Nations Register of Conventional Arms might be the first step towards the creation of a globally respected management system and body of values. But, as suggested earlier, international support for the Register has been slow to develop, its contribution is, at present, marginal, and its future is less secure than might be hoped. Some of this inertia is attributable to commercial pressures, but there are other, more structural difficulties to be considered here. First, there is the matter of national sovereignty – of which so much has been heard and seen since the end of the Cold War – and its contribution to international politics. Second, it would seem that the bank of knowledge and experience has too little to offer those seeking ways to regulate the international arms market which has, so far, suffered from a history of neglect. A huge amount of experience has, however, accumulated in the pursuit of non-proliferation of weapons of mass destruction (WMD). There is a tendency to draw on this WMD experience, but is it easily transferable to the conventional sphere?

Article 51, National Sovereignty and International Law

The end of the Cold War adversarial relationship has removed one important source of structure and control. The passing of the hegemonic, or 'spheres of influence', logic of Cold War arms trading has enabled the development of what might be termed the 'Article 51 argument', referring to Article 51 of the United Nations Charter. But if this is to be the new rationale for the international arms market, it is difficult to see how the result could be more convincing standards of restraint and responsibility than those which obtained during the Cold War. The significance of Article 51 is that it confirms every UN member state's 'inherent right of individual or collective self-defence' against armed attack. As the British government and others have argued, Article 51 could be read to imply that states also have 'the right to acquire the means with which to defend themselves' (House of Commons, para. 24). Comments to this effect have been included in several of the post-Cold War regulatory initiatives. The Article 51 argument is especially relevant for those states which have no indigenous arms industry and which therefore rely on the international market to acquire their means of self-defence. But the Article 51 argument begins to do some damage to the search for a central value or standard by which to organize the international arms trade, and against which to judge national policies. If, like non-intervention, self-defence is a key attribute of sovereignty – which it surely must be – then any interference in that right, even by instituting an arms embargo, undermines to some extent the very *notion* of national sovereignty. National sovereignty is, arguably, the central feature of the international system as it is currently constituted. National sovereignty is an attribute enjoyed and valued as much by those states imposing an arms embargo or trade restriction, as it is by the 'pariah' state or regime which is the 'target' of the punitive action. And if an arms embargo or trade denial is to be legitimized by reference to an 'international community' of *sovereign* states, a contradictory and confusing muddle of means and ends seems unavoidable. If self-defence and, by extension, the arms trade are attributes of sovereignty then a state should expect to be treated by its peers as 'innocent until proven guilty'. That is, a state should be allowed to exercise its self-defence and arms-purchasing rights until good reason emerges why it should not.

The Article 51 argument is a persuasive one, and one which, moreover, carries the force of international law. Indeed, international law serves as a useful model of what can – and cannot – be achieved. To the extent that the primary element of the international political system is the sovereign state, admitting of no superior secular authority or 'world government', then the system could be described as anarchic. But, in the sense conveyed by the expression 'anarchical *society*', the relations between the primary elements of this system conform to predictable patterns and are governed by rules. International lawyers could, therefore, be described as managers or 'facilitators' of this anarchical society, in that they are not practitioners of a supervening rule of law in the domestic sense, but are advocates of a co-operative, contractual law *between* states. A sceptic might see international law as a fragile edifice, contingent upon the continued endorsement of states and little more than normal diplomatic intercourse taken at a more leisurely pace. However, while it is correct to draw distinctions between international law and domestic legal systems, it is important not to jettison the complex and expanding web of international law simply because it takes different approaches and serves different purposes. A more balanced assessment of the practice and value of international law might see it as 'the record of restrictions on sovereignty *accepted by states*', with the law's 'principal function' being to 'overcome the initial presumption of sovereignty and nonintervention' (Donnelly, p.29).

Weapons of Mass Destruction

There is also a technical aspect to the problem of defining an international standard. In recent decades, governments may have begun to see conventional arms transfers as a peripheral issue, if not normal or even preferred practice. This conditioning could be seen as a legacy of the Cold War, when the control of weapons of mass destruction (WMD) and the pressing need to prevent further proliferation of such weapons tended to capture the greater part of government and public imagination. Given the precarious nature of East–West tension during the Cold War, and the vast strategic nuclear arsenals which could have been unleashed had that tension ever developed into open conflict, this bias was to be expected. Not all Cold War arms control was devoted to strategic weaponry. A great deal of effort, for example, went into balancing NATO and Warsaw Pact conventional forces in Europe, culminating in the elaborate treaty on Conventional Armed Forces in Europe (CFE), signed in November 1990 as the East–West confrontation was coming to an end. But conventional arms *transfer* controls were a different matter, and were largely relegated to the second order. Conventional arms transfers may even have been seen as a 'release valve', or a means to continue the Cold War struggle by other, non-WMD means. The WMD/conventional weapons substitution issue continues to be relevant, and may be perceived as an impediment to effective multilateral export control management, insofar as an over-restrictive conventional arms trade regime which had the effect of pushing the 'target' state towards WMD acquisition would probably be seen as counter-productive.

Could the lessons of WMD non-proliferation have more immediate application? With relatively clear and convincing (albeit not universally accepted) sets of norms having been developed to accompany the various WMD non-proliferation initiatives, there is perhaps an understandable temptation to assume that something similar ought to be available in the sphere of conventional arms and technology transfers.

But controlling the trade in conventional arms and technology differs from WMD non-proliferation schemes in several respects, and these differences underscore the difficulty of establishing convincing, internationally acceptable norms for arms trade restraint. First, although the risks which may accompany the acquisition of a large conventional arsenal ought not to be underestimated, these risks are best understood in local or at most regional terms. This same complacency could, however, prove to be wholly misplaced with regard to the acquisition by some states of weapons of mass destruction. Nuclear, biological and chemical weaponry, and ballistic missiles, have been defined as 'catastrophic weaponry', weapons which would, if used, 'necessarily devastate civilian populations with catastrophic consequences' (Kellman, p.757). Simply put; 'the global threat from states acquiring more conventional arms is qualitatively different from that of the same states acquiring nuclear armaments' (Simpson, p.231). Another distinction lies in the character of the weapons. Weapons of mass destruction are often perceived and described in absolute terms; strategically, politically, legally and morally. These perceptions have so far exerted a powerful influence upon decisions regarding the development, possession and possible use of WMD. But it is more difficult to say similar things of conventional weapons. The manufacture, ownership and deployment of conventional weapons are more readily understood to be a working extension of international politics – even into warfare – whereas WMD threaten the complete and final negation of political discourse. Although it must be correct to say that in some circumstances, certain weapons can be 'destabilizing' or 'decisive', or offer an 'offensive' capability, it is difficult to apply these definitions in a categorical way where conventional weapons are concerned. The technical capabilities of a given conventional weapons system are available to the possessor to exploit, in aggression as in defence; 'destabilizing' and 'offensive' are therefore judgements which are best made in context. For a military commander in a defensive position, the vital task is to steal the initiative from the aggressor, and some weapons, such as tanks, which would be invaluable for an aggressor, could be used legitimately for this purpose. A conventional confrontation is often as much about the initiative and ability of the military commander as it is about the quantity and quality of the weapons being deployed. On many occasions, being on equal terms in armaments, or even being the underdog, has had little bearing on military decisions. Indeed, some military commanders appear to view qualitative and quantitative disadvantage as a challenge to be met, and rather relish acting the role of David outsmarting Goliath. The performance of the Israeli armed forces on the Golan Heights in 1973 is often cited in this respect, but a more recent example of the triumph of self-confidence over military capability might be the

Chechen rebels' struggle against Russian armour and air power in late 1994 and 1995. It is also relevant to note that US and NATO military doctrine underwent a 'revolution' in the 1980s and early 1990s, the result of which was a deliberate blurring of offensive and defensive in military planning and operations (Toffler, p. 62).

The final distinction to be drawn between the conventional arms trade and the proliferation of weapons of mass destruction is one which recalls the precepts of academic theory about the organization and functioning of international regimes on the one hand, and the facts of a diffuse and possibly uncontrollable world-wide conventional arms and technology production base on the other. As the conventional armaments production base broadens, so it must become more difficult to control; 'multilateral efforts at controls can be effective only when the objects of controls are wholly within the influence orbit of those seeking to implement them' (Harkavy, p.220). On a more theoretical level, industrial and technological diffusion also undermines one of the principles of effective non-proliferation: that 'deviants' should be kept 'small in number, isolated, and manageable' (Chafetz, p.146). These practical and theoretical stipulations might be relevant in the field of WMD proliferation, but they seem scarcely appropriate for the post-Cold War conventional arms market.

Three Choices

The diffuse post-Cold War international order, combined with a legacy of relative indifference to the spread of conventional weapons, and the inappropriateness of WMD non-proliferation models, offers three choices, none of them especially convincing as a central organizing principle or mechanism. First, the 'Article 51 argument' could be taken to mean that the international arms trade can only be judged in relative or regional terms; an overarching, absolute and universally applicable set of values is logically, politically and morally unattainable. A second choice could be to apply a version of the Cold War 'release valve' idea and argue that the international arms trade ought still, in certain circumstances, to be encouraged. The priority would be to ensure that states are not persuaded that their goals could be realized through the acquisition of WMD. This argument could also extend into the idea that states have a moral obligation to transfer arms to those engaged in self-defence against an aggressor. There is a compelling simplicity to both the 'Article 51' and the 'release valve' arguments. But both arguments entail a presumption of access to the arms market rather than restraint of it. It would appear, therefore, that in adhering to either of these arguments the very considerations – pragmatic, legal and moral – which prompt states to control and restrain the market nationally and multilaterally would have to be compromised in some way.

A third option could be to argue that while self-defence is indeed a right of states, it is not an absolute right but one which must instead be enjoyed within the rule-based international legal and political system. More importantly, one state's right to self-defence should not entail an *unqualified* moral and legal *obligation* on other states to export weapons, except perhaps where there is a treaty requirement to assist or defend allies. Arms and technology export proposals should therefore be examined on their merits, on a 'case-by-case' basis; this has been the position adopted by the British and other arms-exporting governments. But if the best that can be said is that 'decisions must be made', then the third option is more a restatement of the problem, rather than a solution to it.

CLASHING CIVILIZATIONS

There are practical, political and technical difficulties in establishing regimes by which the conventional arms and technology trade might be controlled. These structural difficulties should offer few surprises; the constraints imposed upon cosmopolitanism by a system of sovereign states, and the character and limitations of international law, are familiar enough. But, probing more deeply, there are also questions to be asked about the logical – and even moral – qualities of any political exercise which, tacitly or otherwise, rests on assumptions which *purport* to be universally valid. Neither are these questions new, however; the possibility of there being absolute truths, values and explanations for things and events has been discussed since at least the time of the classical Greek philosophers. If something can be said to be absolute, must it not also be universally valid? But if so, how can apparent exceptions be explained? Aristotle noticed that 'fire burns both in Hellas and Persia; but men's ideas of right and wrong vary from place to place.' Rather more recently, in his 1906 play *Major Barbara*, George Bernard Shaw put similar lines in the mouth of Andrew Undershaft, the fictional arms manufacturer: 'For me there is only one true morality; but it might not fit you, as you do not manufacture aerial battleships. There is only one true morality for every man; but every man has not the same true morality' (Act 1). Since the European Enlightenment, Western thinkers, wrestling with their increasing awareness of the uncomfortable reality of a heterogeneous world, have grappled with this problem and have debated the notion of historical and cultural 'relativism'.

But what is becoming increasingly apparent, after the Cold War, is that these questions and misgivings are no longer exclusively the substance of an internal debate among Western political philosophers. Challenges to Western universalist assumptions no longer need to be made theoretically and vicariously, on behalf of other cultures and traditions; there are now more than enough vocal, non-Western critics of these Western assumptions. As far as the international arms market is concerned, it is becoming increasingly difficult – practically and logically – to ignore the opinions of non-participants in, late arrivals at, or even targets of Western attempts at, regime-building, supervision and control. The problem becomes most pronounced when the arms and technology recipients with the most awkward questions about the rationale for embargoes and technology denial, are at the same time enjoying the benefits of the buyer's market discussed in Chapter 2 and are therefore in a position to 'vote with their feet'. Tension mounts when the rationale and machinery of export regulation are perceived by the thwarted or prospective client to be extensions of the cultural values of those setting out to supervise or regulate the arms trade – a group of Western arms suppliers, for example. These values may be understood by the suppliers to be absolute values, but may not be accepted in the same way by the recipients, or for that matter by other supplier governments of a different political or cultural persuasion and in a position to fill any gaps in the market. The tension is greatest when the linkage becomes prescriptive, with the suppliers' values being presented as norms and standards of behaviour to which all states should aspire. Dissatisfied clients might argue that conditions should not be imposed which are alien to their country's cultural tradition and outlook or beyond the political and economic scope of their government, perhaps because constitutional government is in its infancy and vulnerable to opponents. Frustrated arms purchasers might also object to what they perceive to be straightforward international power politics. If all the language of democracy, human rights, individual freedoms and so forth is in reality little more than a cynical attempt to dignify hegemonic practices, then states on the supply-side of the arms market could be accused actually of having too little respect for the abstract principles of sovereign equality of states and for the right of self-defence, with which they identify so closely.

The Humbled West?

In his 1952 Reith Lectures for the BBC, the British historian Arnold Toynbee spoke of the 'encounter between the World and the West' and warned of the limited acceptance of the Western world-view:

> A Westerner who wants to grapple with this subject, must try, for a few minutes, to slip out of his native Western skin and look at the encounter between the world and the West through the eyes of the great non-Western majority of mankind. Different though the non-Western peoples of the world may be from one another in race, language, civilization, and religion, if any Western inquirer asks them their opinion of the West, he will hear them all giving him the same answer: Russians, Muslims, Hindus, Chinese, Japanese, and all the rest. The West, they will tell him, has been the arch-aggressor of modern times, and each will have their own experience of Western aggression to bring up against him (Toynbee, p. 2).

More recently, a summary of the dilemma and evidence of growing sensitivity to these issues in the West, was provided in early 1995, in a report by an influential US research institute, the Institute for National Security Studies (INSS). The report noted that while 'the global advancement of democracy and respect for human rights' had made 'notable strides' in the 1980s, the experience of the 1990s and the immediate prospects were less encouraging (INSS, p.187). Although conditions were generally improving around the world, the report noted that 'democratic ideals' were in some cases being observed only perfunctorily. Since the end of the Cold War, these ideals had come under 'severe pressure' in many of the 'new democracies'. In some cases, the explanation was to be found in a clash of priorities: 'Many new democracies have discovered problems in reconciling group rights and individual freedom with political stability. Severe contractions of national economies have frequently turned public opinion against democratic reformers who were raised to leadership in the wake of the Soviet Union's disintegration, most notably in Russia itself.' Other explanations offered in the report for the uneven application of democratic principles included the surge in nationalist feeling, awakened by improvements in communications and education, the close connection in some areas between political and religious movements, and the belief that religion, ethnicity and 'group consensus' were values which mattered more than democratic ambitions. But the report also argued that the spread of democracy had in some senses been too successful, that democratic values had been spread too thin, and that 'With the global diffusion of democracy, it has become clear that what is meant by 'democracy' varies from state to state as a result of differing cultural influences.'

The INSS report could be seen as part of a developing trend in which Western scholars are themselves challenging comfortable Western ideas and assumptions about the dynamics of the post-Cold War international order. In 1993, for example, the British military historian John Keegan published *A History of Warfare*, in which he argued that warfare itself could only be understood in relative terms, as an expression of idiosyncratic cultural structures and preferences. He found the resort to war, and conduct in war, to be subjects rather more complex than had been realized in the West, and more diffuse than would be admitted by Western devotees of Clausewitz, the eighteenth century Prussian military philosopher so admired in Western military academies:

> Culture is ... a prime determinant of the nature of warfare, as the history of its development in Asia clearly demonstrates. Oriental warmaking, if we may so identify and denominate it as something different and apart from European warfare, is characterised by traits peculiar to itself. [...] Future peacekeepers and peacemakers have much to learn from alternative military cultures, not only that of the Orient, but of the primitive world also (Keegan, pp.387, 392.)

Another example of the trend was an article, also published in 1993, by Samuel Huntington, an American political scientist. Huntington's article – in many respects an important illustration of new tensions and problems that have arisen since the end of the Cold War – was controversial and somewhat alarmist, meeting vigorous challenge from a number of quarters. Huntington began his article by identifying the 'fundamental source of conflict' which, in his view, would not be 'primarily ideological or primarily economic. The great divisions among humankind and the dominating source of conflict will be cultural.' Huntington described a non-Western world no longer willing to be 'the objects of history as the targets of Western colonialism' and keen to join the West as 'movers and shapers of history' (Huntington, [A] p.23). He found that the West had made use of ill-defined notions such as 'world community' and 'universal civilization' to legitimize the spread of Western values and preferences, political, economic and moral. Not only was the idea of a universal civilization at odds with 'the particularism of most Asian societies', but the values being presented also 'differed fundamentally' from those found in other civilizations: 'Western ideas of individualism, liberalism, constitutionalism, human rights, equality, liberty, the rule of law, democracy, free markets, the separation of church and state, often have little resonance in Islamic, Confucian, Japanese, Hindu, Buddhist or Orthodox cultures' (p.40). More ominously, perhaps, he also applied his thesis to security matters and the spread of conventional arms and technology. While most Western countries were reducing military spending and military power, many in the Middle East and Asia–Pacific regions were moving in the opposite direction, asserting their 'right to acquire and to deploy whatever weapons they think necessary for their security.' In response to this loss of control, Huntington saw the West attempting to use arms control – 'a Western concept and a Western goal' – along with political and economic pressure to prevent the development of 'military capabilities that could threaten Western interests.' But Huntington was not overly optimistic in this regard; he saw the states of the Middle East and the Asia-Pacific rim developing a 'Confucian–Islamic military connection ... designed to promote acquisition by its members of the weapons and weapons technologies needed to counter the military power of the West' (p.47).

Huntington provoked lively debate and criticism, some rather pointed. One critic, for example, described Huntington's ideas as a 'mushy amalgam, and a bundle of unexplored and dubious connections between religion, culture, civilisation, state and strife' (Hoffman, p.32). Others chastised Huntington for over-estimating the clarity and validity of 'civilization' as an organizing concept in international politics and – somewhat unfairly – for under-estimating the central importance of the state in the international system; nations would not 'battle for civilizational ties and fidelities when they would rather scramble for their market shares, learn how to compete in a merciless world economy, provide ideas, move out of poverty' (Ajami, p.5). Another critic – a senior Singaporean diplomat – rejected as alarmism the idea of a discrete, coherent Islamic force ('fundamental' or otherwise), rubbished Huntington's notion of a 'Confucian–Islamic' connection in matters of military security and arms sales, and also questioned whether 'Western civilization' had sufficient coherence and integrity to merit the label (Mahbubani).

Huntington made a spirited response to his critics. He argued again that 'What ultimately counts for people is not political ideology or economic interest. Faith and family, blood and belief, are what people identify with and what they will fight and die for' (Huntington [B]). This is not an especially contentious point of view, although some might still argue that 'economic interest' is more significant than Huntington would allow. Somewhat more contentious was his claim that 'the clash of civilizations is replacing the Cold War as the central phenomenon of global politics.' Here, Huntington could be charged with conflating the general context, in which political decisions are made and behaviour takes place, with the contingent and particular motives which inform those decisions and drive that behaviour. It is one thing for individual and national political behaviour to be, in some general sense, *civilizational*, but rather another for actions to be guided by direct reference or appeal to *civilization* itself. Nevertheless, for the purposes of this book there is an important lesson to be drawn from the analysis of Keegan, Huntington and others: simply that arrangements or codes of behaviour which aspire to be valid across the international system of states, yet which are based upon assumptions which may not be accepted in all states, may prove to have unsteady foundations.

Relativism, and with it a sense of humility and proportion, could therefore be an appropriate tool for both describing and understanding the more diffuse and heterogeneous post-Cold War world. Rather than assume that Western values and practices will be accepted universally and automatically, the Western value system should be placed alongside other equally respectable and valid systems and cultures. This open-minded and mature approach does, however, create practical problems for the implementation of political systems and procedures which appear to derive some or all of their authority and legitimacy from a value system which has the aura of universal validity, but which can no longer be assumed to have that quality, even by its closest adherents. That being said, it does not follow that *any* idea or procedure that can be shown to have been derived from a given value-system or cultural tradition must be discarded as being unfit for international consumption; were this the case, relativism and open-mindedness would have given way to moral, political and intellectual paralysis. A more subtle approach is called for. Values may be absolute, pure and true, but if these values apply only in one small corner of the earth's surface, under siege by alternative visions of the world and its future, then it is difficult to see how these values could be supposed to have anything more than local relevance. The search for a satisfactory blend of absolutism and universalism has long entertained political philosophers, and is not about to reach its conclusion here. One way to break through this dilemma is to search out the common ground which lies *between* different value-systems; it may be that one political procedure or area of international co-operation could be consonant with the ideas and values of different systems. The essential point – and it is perhaps no more than a matter of language and perceptions – is not to assume from the outset that cultural mores can translate swiftly and easily into universally applicable political systems. Rather, it may only be possible to build these systems where the world's different value-systems overlap.

Yet subtlety and discretion have been scarce commodities in the various post-Cold War attempts to supervise or control the conventional arms trade. The UN Register of Conventional Arms emerges as the most neutral and even-handed, and the least 'judgmental'. But the Register is more a supervisory than a regulatory initiative. Participation is entirely voluntary and 'requires' no more of states than the reporting of certain information. The Register has the support of a significant number of states, if not yet enough to realize its potential as a global confidence-building measure. Yet it may be that the level of support for the Register that has been achieved to date has been at the expense of real authority. In other words, as participation in the Register has broadened, the process has remained coherent only by becoming shallower and less exacting. Both the P5 and G7 initiatives of 1991, however, went beyond the relatively uncontroversial goal of restricting aggression and breaches of international peace and security to use such expressions as 'legitimate self-defence' when referring to potential recipients. From the recipient's point of view, expressions of this nature begin to suggest that the right of self-defence has become less an attribute of state sovereignty – one which could be described as absolute and inalienable within the parameters of international law, than a quality that can be defined, awarded or denied by a state's peers within the international system. The CSCE's November 1993 'Principles Governing Conventional Arms Transfers' went one step further and mentioned 'the respect for human rights and fundamental freedoms in the recipient country', as well as 'legitimate security and defence needs', as criteria against which potential conventional arms purchasers should be judged. The European Union's eight 'criteria' were an earlier articulation of some of the same thinking. And in 1995, in a similar vein, the International Committee of the Red Cross began to investigate the possibility of linking arms transfer decisions to a potential recipient's compliance with the international humanitarian law of armed conflict.

The Assertive Rest?

The facts of the buyer's market, and the logic of the 'Article 51 argument', already make it possible in a practical sense for recipient states to challenge the tactic, as they might perceive it, of 'hegemony by stealth' by the arms and technology supplier states. Is there a sub-text or 'hidden agenda' behind arms trade restrictions which has more to do with economic and military power and dominance than with cultural values? And any attempt to interfere with the conventional arms market, even an arms embargo, raises questions both about the structure of the international system and about the sources of authority and legitimacy – political and moral – within that system. These questions become more urgent when interference in the arms market is accompanied by a rationale which is claimed to be universally valid. Which is the main, organizing principle in the international system: the sovereign authority of individual states, or the supposed universality of interests and values perceived by many to be characteristically *Western*? Prescriptive linkages may be made, as in the CSCE/OSCE and European Union initiatives, but is it reasonable to assume that ideas such as human rights, individual freedom, democracy and so forth are both generally accepted and appreciated, as well as uniformly applicable around the world. Even if these values could be defined and accepted as universal, some would see them as ideals rather than policy prescriptions, with some states requiring more time to realize these goals while remaining stable and secure.

In May 1993, at about the time Huntington's 'Clash of Civilizations' article appeared, Asian nations assembled in Bangkok to issue a new definition of human rights, one which stressed social stability and economic development over individual freedoms. Ideas of this sort continue to be heard, particularly in the Asia–Pacific region and in Southeast Asia. Malaysia's prime minister, Dr Mahathir Mohamad, became an especially outspoken critic of Western attempts to proselytize:

No one, no country, no people and no civilization has a
right to claim it has a monopoly of wisdom as to what
constitute human rights ... [Western liberals] have no right
at all to talk of human rights, much less judge others on this
issue. ... The record of the democratic governments of the
West is not very inspiring. Unless their own interests are at
stake, as in Kuwait, they would not risk anything in the
cause of democracy. Is it any wonder that many countries
are leery of the liberal system propounded by the Western
democrats? [1]

Mahathir earlier gained notoriety for his angry response to British
media accusations regarding the Pergau Dam 'trade and aid' scandal,
a response which was particularly relevant to discussion of the arms
trade and its regulation. In a letter to the *Financial Times*, Mahathir
declared that 'Malaysians are not concerned about British scruples
over selling arms .... If you have scruples, don't sell arms at all.'[2] In
July 1995 Malaysia was one of the leading Organisation of Islamic
Conference states to declare the UN arms embargo on Bosnia
invalid, and to offer military supplies to aid the Bosnian Muslims.[3]

Malaysia's close neighbour Singapore, also with close ties with the
West, has been similarly critical. Outcry following a legal case in
which the *International Herald Tribune* was found guilty of contempt
of court, prompted Singapore's High Commissioner in London to
publish his view that 'democracy is a long process and, in the short
term, it is better perhaps to have more prosperity than democracy,'
and to note that 'Dogmatic assertions that Western democracy will
inevitably triumph over Asian values only reminds Asians of the
fervour with which Communists once proclaimed the inevitable
triumph of Communism.' And following the collapse of a British
merchant bank in March 1995, the same High Commissioner
chastised *The Economist* for assuming that 'London bankers are the

only people who have the integrity and ability to regulate and operate foreign exchanges. When a vulnerable British bank collapses it is not wise to blame it on regulatory failure on the part of your former colonial subjects – and their institutions – without checking the facts. Hubris indeed.'[4] Indeed, Singapore is host to the so-called Singapore school of human rights lawyers and thinkers who argue the need for social stability and economic growth and who place 'the interests of the majority prior to the rights of the individual' (Chew, p.934).

The People's Republic of China has long argued along similar lines. For the PRC, sovereignty and non-intervention have always been declared to be the irreducible core of relations between states. Thus, in January 1995, following a US report on human rights abuses in the PRC, the Chinese response was to argue that 'The human rights issue is within the scope of the sovereignty of a country. Every country has the right to protect and promote human rights in accordance with its own situation.'[5] By one account, even the PRC's radical intellectuals had come to accept that the 'military crackdown' in June 1989 was necessary and were supportive of Deng Xiaoping's view that the Soviet Union's attempt to achieve economic liberalization and political liberalism simultaneously was not an example which the PRC should attempt to follow.[6]

If, as is apparent from arguments of the sort advanced by Malaysia, Singapore and the PRC, the universal and unconditional acceptance of predominantly Western standards cannot be assumed, then it follows that political arrangements which draw upon – or merely make reference to – these standards could also be open to challenge. In these circumstances, discussion of the universality of human rights and democratic values could become an abstract and possibly counter-productive preoccupation. If the arrangement is one which simply and explicitly requires states to meet Western preferred standards of behaviour before, for example, commercial relationships can develop, then it is open for non-Western states to choose whether to comply with or reject that requirement, just as it is open for Western states to make such stipulations in the first instance. But these same standards assume a more rigid, prescriptive and controversial air when they are presented as universal values. At best, the outcome might then be reduced scope for successful commercial relationships between states with different cultural systems. At worst, the result could be a perception of Western proselytizing and 'hegemony by stealth'; a tacit attempt to undermine national sovereign authority. Among the many technical and procedural objections to the Wassenaar Arrangement, the following comments were attributed to an Iranian official:

> We don't think that ad hoc arrangements discussed among a club of Western countries, European countries is workable...It would lead to confrontation between South and North... We think the best way to control military technology or dual-use technology is through universal agreement... [participating countries] have come up with a self-serving arrangement which is being operated on a discriminatory basis.[7]

Although these differences of opinion between 'the West' and 'the Rest' must be acknowledged, it is important not to become caught up in rhetoric which may be designed more for domestic consumption, and to ignore the many commercial and political relationships which do bridge the supposed chasms between civilizations. There is plenty of evidence, for example, that Western governments are as aware of their trade figures as they are keen to improve standards of human rights and governance around the world. And there is also an argument that restrictions on trade can worsen the condition of individuals already suffering under abusive regimes. In March 1995, at the UN social summit in Copenhagen, representatives of the British government questioned the idea of cutting trade with countries with poor human rights records and argued that free trade was the key to global prosperity and the elimination of poverty.[8] In July 1995 Germany 'put human rights issues aside' and signed £2 billion worth of industrial contracts with the PRC.[9] But perhaps most telling of all, given the involvement of the European Commission in efforts to standardize European arms and technology export control practices, and to have those practices informed by human rights and other criteria, was the Commission's advice to European Union leaders in February 1996 'to avoid needling Asian sensitivities over human rights when they meet the region's statesmen in Bangkok... for a summit to pave the way to new trading and political bonds.'[10] There is also evidence that non-Western states and cultures can accept both the principle of universalism and overlook the cultural ancestry of certain ideas, and are by no means unfamiliar with the idea of a general, world-wide code of behaviour. The idea of human rights, for example, could be described as being of Western origin. It is also an idea which, self-evidently, aspires to be universally applied. Yet in spite of its origins and its apparent scope, most states have at least accepted international definitions of human rights, even to the extent of being bound in international treaty law.

Serious differences can occur, however, when the *sine qua non* of national sovereignty, and, by extension, the expectation of non-intervention and the right of self-defence, are all perceived to be threatened in some way. The quarrel with attempts to link arms and technology transfers with ideas such as human rights might be, therefore, neither with the origins (e.g., Western) of the idea (e.g., human rights), nor with its supposed scope (e.g., universal). The issue, instead, might be a more straightforward one of power and authority. International law can be understood as mitigating the exercise of state sovereignty, without conflicting in essential terms with the ideas of states and their sovereignty. Concepts such as human rights, democracy and individual freedoms only become objectionable when some attempt is made to implement them. At this point, mere ideas become subversive norms, which are perceived to cut across and intrude upon sovereignty and which, unlike international law, challenge the presumption that state sovereignty lies at the centre of all things international. States may agree upon definitions of human rights, but may also reserve the right, as sovereign members of the international community, to decide where, when and by whom these political goals should be realized. Unlike international law which is, in some respects, the servant of sovereignty, 'The universality of human rights fits uncomfortably in a political order structured around sovereign states' (Donnelly, p.30). Furthermore, as discussed earlier, the sacrosanct nature of national sovereignty becomes assailed from two directions when the 'Article 51' right to self-defence is made conditional upon good behaviour domestically.

CONCLUSION

In response to these dilemmas, pragmatic governments on the supply side of the international arms market, bombarded by the demands of their electorate for more 'principled' policies, may wish to find some way to distinguish between absolute and universal, and may find refuge in expressions such as 'weak cultural relativism' or 'relative universality' (Donnelly, p.35; Cassese, p.50). For, as far as the international market for arms and related technology is concerned, the awkward reality will remain that many non-Western countries now feel themselves in a position to decide, on their own terms and for their own applications, what is meant by human rights, freedom and good government. Western countries still have some means to compel Third World and developing countries to behave in certain ways, usually by attaching conditions to aid and investment provisions. And for the most egregious offences against Western opinion and standards of behaviour there are various types of embargo and economic sanction, and even military action. But arms transfer controls have not been a great success as a tool of coercive diplomacy, and in any case coercion hardly seems the stuff of which a global arms trade ethic and code of conduct could be made. Furthermore, as the Asia–Pacific region and Southeast Asia become ever more technologically and commercially dynamic and wealthy, and therefore attractive to Western investors, so it seems increasingly unwise for the West to insist upon the transcendence of values and standards which its potential commercial partners evidently do not share. Western self-confidence is least appropriate in the case of conventional arms and technology transfers. Networks of arms sales and weapons development projects already stretch from the Middle East to the Asia–Pacific rim. With the inauguration in January 1995 of the Malaysia–Singapore Defence Forum, one object of which will be to enhance defence-related industrial collaboration between the two countries, and with Singapore also offering defence-related industrial management expertise to the PRC, it would appear that something similar to Huntington's 'Islamic–Confucian' connection could indeed be developing. In these circumstances, attempts by the West, or by the so-called supply-side, to make conventional arms and technology transfers conditional, could be viewed as culturally and morally arrogant and could prove to be commercially counter-productive.

NOTES

1. 'Dr Mahathir and Malaysia's Diplomatic Agenda', *Asian Defence and Diplomacy*, January 1995.
2. Letters, *Financial Times*, 17 March 1994.
3. 'Muslim world to arm Bosnians', *The Times*, 24 July 1995.
4. Letters, *The Economist*, 25 March 1995.
5. 'China tells US not to meddle', *The Times*, 3 February 1995.
6. 'But the people of China have a stake in the status quo', *The Japan Times*, 11 January 1995.
7. 'Wassenaar Arrangement controversial', *BASIC Reports*, 21 February 1996.
8. 'Britain urges UN to drop trade and human rights link', *The Times*, 11 March 1995.
9. 'Trade takes priority over human rights', *Daily Telegraph*, 15 July 1995.
10. 'EU warned not to push rights issue at Asian summit', *The Times*, 28 February 1996.

5

CONCLUSION

This book set out to explain the shape, size and dynamics of the post-Cold War international conventional arms trade, and to show why and how states should wish to control the flow of conventional arms, military equipment and related technology. International efforts to reduce – or merely manage – the global trade in conventional weapons, equipment and related technology have so far had an indifferent record. Multilateral arms and technology embargoes, or restricted access regimes, have been used frequently, sometimes to great effect. But conventional arms embargoes and the like are best understood as ad hoc responses to changing political and strategic circumstances. It is difficult to see how this mould might be broken, with the market being shaped in an anticipatory way by the disinterested, but no less dynamic, will of what is sometimes rather wistfully referred to as the 'international community'.

For 45 years after the end of World War II, the international arms trade was dominated by the East-West confrontation, and the trade expanded dramatically during these years. As far as regulation of the market is concerned, the best that might be said of the Cold War is that it imposed some sense of order and predictability. The 1990s have seen rapid contraction in the global market from the post-war peak in the late 1980s. But in the absence of the rudimentary discipline of the Cold War, with the spread of arms manufacturing and technological capability, and with the arrival of a buyer's market for conventional military equipment and related technology, the shrinking market of the 1990s has become less ordered and less predictable. As a result, recent initiatives to bring the arms trade under some form of international control could well share the ignominious fate of similar attempts made earlier this century.

But the starting point for this brief study was to ask why there should be a market for conventional weapons in the first place. The traditional response to this question is in terms of *threat perceptions*, the right to *self-defence* and so forth. Interestingly, when aggressive intent is disguised, and when military adventurism develops suddenly and without warning, the justification for the international arms trade might seem to be at its most urgent and persuasive. Yet, given that arms contracts usually take many years – even decades – to negotiate and complete, this moment of greatest urgency can also be the time when the arms trade is least timely and relevant, with the suppliers simply unable to meet their customers' vital needs. This points to an important feature of the international arms market: the rationale for official trading in arms and military equipment is seldom – if ever – discrete, transparent and uncontroversial. Instead, the logic in many cases amounts to a rather untidy collection of imperfect impressions and questionable contingency plans. With all this untidiness, and with the mere possibility that policies might have been ill-chosen, the result can be heated domestic debate, where such things are possible. What is more, there is the matter of the so-called security dilemma: the risk that involvement in the arms trade might create the very problem to which arms imports were originally thought to be a response. Developing countries need access to technology for their general industrial and economic improvement. It is often claimed that one route to such technology acquisition lies in the arms trade. But this argument must also be treated with caution. The non-military benefits of military spending by developing countries appear to be marginal, while the opportunity costs can be very high.

A common explanation for the motive to export arms is the health of a state's defence-related industrial sector. In some respects, a healthy defence industry can be as important as well-equipped and well-prepared armed forces. Defence industry is often described as 'vital' or a 'strategic national asset'. But, with industrial internationalization, the spread of technology and the 'civilianization' of innovation, there is increasing cause to question the notion that defence industry can be considered a self-contained national possession. Another explanation lies in the realm of foreign policy. The claim that arms exports can be a legitimate tool – or even end – of foreign policy arouses particular controversy. Yet the foreign policy perspective is becoming increasingly fragile, given the growing numbers of alternative suppliers willing to enter the post-Cold War buyer's market for arms.

The size of this market is notoriously difficult to estimate, partly because the market involves activity which is politically secretive and commercially sensitive. Nevertheless, there is wide agreement that the international market for conventional weapons has contracted dramatically since the mid-1980s. A small group of suppliers – mainly Western – dominate the market, and the Middle East is the largest arms-importing region. But the most important feature of the post-Cold War arms market is not who is selling what, to whom, but that the market is becoming much more diffuse. What we see is a dramatically reduced market in which the initiative has moved very significantly in the direction of the buyer. This has the effect of diluting the potential of the supply-side to control the market. The internationalization of defence industry and the 'civilianization' of innovation can be seen to have a broadly similar, loosening effect. The rather pessimistic conclusion from these observations, made in Chapter 2, was that 'technology denial and export control policies face an uphill struggle.'

Nevertheless, the arms trade is still something that states seek to control. Indeed, it could be argued that a state which does not seek to control the arms trade has failed to grasp the qualities and responsibilities of statehood, not least the imperative of self-preservation. Chapter 3 offered several explanations for this creed of control, and described some of the main initiatives which have been made, nationally and internationally. Strategic/pragmatic, legal and ethical imperatives can be identified which drive states both to create some form of national export control system and, subsequently, to join with other governments in multinational control efforts. Chapter 3 acknowledged the established wisdom that for control to be effective and worth pursuing, it must be multilateral and involve all or many suppliers and, if possible, the principal recipients; the perception that 'a unilateral defence sales embargo ... would amount to little more than counter productive gesture politics' (Masefield, p.15), persuades governments that their national goals might best – or only – be achieved in some multilateral framework.

Yet there must be difficulties when the object to be regulated and supervised is not completely within the grasp or competence of those seeking to exercise control. Some of the observations made in Chapter 2 regarding the spread of defence manufacturing capability around the world, and the tempo of the essentially innocent processes of experimentation and innovation, point in this direction. But Chapter 4 revealed the problem of control to be conceptual as well as technological. Put simply, the value-system which accompanies and legitimizes most – if not all – post-Cold War control initiatives is perceived by many important customers in the market-place to be alien to their tradition and culture. And with the market changing and becoming more diffuse, dissatisfaction with the merchant's packaging can swiftly and easily lead to the customer taking his business elsewhere, to those suppliers who can provide weapons, military equipment and technology without unwelcome political, moral and cultural lecturing. Attempts to organize the international arms market along the lines of recognizably *Western* values and standards of behaviour can only be vitiated by arguments such as that advanced in mid-1995 by the Prime Minister of Malaysia: 'Malaysians are not concerned about British scruples over selling arms ... If you have scruples, don't sell arms at all.'

The rather bleak vision presented by this book suggests various policy alternatives. First, the pessimistic outlook could be accepted at face value and the idea that the control of the international arms market should reflect some higher, objective set of values – ethical or otherwise – could be abandoned altogether. There might still be scope for principled national decision-making, and even for co-operation with like-minded states. But the determined projection of demonstrably Western values would not be attempted, and the international arms trade would have to be understood as a global problem without a global answer. Yet the risk with this approach is that the very idea of regulation, either national or multilateral, would then prove unsustainable in the face of the argument 'if we don't export, others will'. And this would in turn undermine the basic pragmatic, legal and moral considerations which initially persuade governments that the arms trade should be regulated, and which then draw them into seeking some form of multilateral co-operation. If there is a need for self-restraint, there is also – arguably – a need to find some means by which self-denial can be legitimized and explained. Since arms trade hegemony and technology denial are either unfashionable or inappropriate, the discussion returns in the end to the seemingly hopeless search for a generally acceptable set of values.

An alternative course might be to reject gloomy scepticism altogether and argue that, whatever the difficulties, the arms trade is something which cannot be left unregulated or badly supervised. By this argument, it is not enough merely to be 'realistic' about the arms trade and accept that it is essentially ungovernable; a badly managed arms trade is a dangerous phenomenon which undermines the very foundations of the international system of states. Out of self-interest alone, if no higher motive is persuasive, states should work towards bringing the market under ever closer control. Regulation of the market can be made rational and effective only by including as many suppliers and clients as possible. And in order to bind these different states together, co-operation should indeed be guided by objective principles such as human rights, democratic freedoms and so on.

But the evidence of this book suggests that this approach might have minimal political effect, at least for the foreseeable future. If, as current circumstances suggest, a 'high-minded and wide-minded' approach to regulating the arms trade is unlikely to be able to overturn the various practical and conceptual obstacles, then the same self-interested imperative to prevent the international arms market becoming entirely ungoverned begins to direct governments towards some less ambitious but potentially more productive strategy. Another problem with refusal to acknowledge the warnings of the sceptics is that it may unwittingly make way for a still more cynical approach to arms trade regulation. We may continue to hold to the idea that the only way to bring the international arms market under control is to seek a broad base of participation among suppliers and recipients. We may, further, argue that co-operation of this sort can only be effective if the participants can legitimize their self-denial in terms of a universally acceptable code of conduct or set of principles. But we already know that a universal code is hard to define and harder still to activate. We could therefore, perversely, be making it easier for less scrupulous governments to pay lip-service to the idea of multilateral arms trade regulation while carrying on with business as usual.

A third option is to search for a middle way between pessimism and idealism; a way which seeks to regulate the international arms trade to the extent that any regulation is possible, even if the result must be incomplete and perhaps short-lived. By this view, objective values can indeed be applied, but only if it is accepted that universal tolerance of these values is not a necessary precondition before any control can be attempted. Thus, a group of suppliers might decide to apply conditions regarding human rights, democratic process, government spending levels and so forth to any of their defence exports, but would do so entirely out of their own conviction, seeking no external legitimation. Conditionality of this sort would still be unlikely to appeal to many potential buyers and would present a market opportunity for other suppliers. 'If we don't export, others will' would therefore remain a potent counter-argument; but then the facts of a buyer's market, and the buyer's new-found self-confidence in world politics, suggest that it always will be. What this approach might however do is make it possible for a limited number of suppliers to act in concert and achieve some – if not all – of the benefits of multilateral co-operation. It may also enable other suppliers and recipients to understand the motives of the collaborating governments and decide, on a more informed and detached basis, whether or not to join in regulating the arms trade.

If standards of behaviour are to be at all convincing and respected, but cannot usefully be portrayed as universal, they should at least exhibit the cultural and moral preferences of the society or group of states which advocates them. As far as regulation of the arms trade is concerned, this extends into the argument that the political level at which strategic, commercial and foreign policy decisions are made regarding the arms trade, should also be the level from which the accompanying values and standards are drawn. By this argument,

the central difficulty with several of the post-Cold War regulatory
initiatives lies not in the attempt to apply objective standards to the
arms trade, but in applying standards inappropriate to the level of
politics at which arms trade decisions are made. Inasmuch as the
arms trade can be made a principled activity, the first step towards
achieving that goal is to ensure that the practical decision-making
process, and the inquiry from principle, take place on the same level,
and in parallel. Some argue that this confluence may be a reasonable
expectation *nationally*, but not *internationally*. If, as this book has
suggested, an important dynamic of the current arms trade is a new-
found sense of self-confidence within the demand-side, freed from
the rigours of the Cold War, then it might be appropriate to
'renationalize' the control of the arms trade, in the way that the
dynamic behind the market also appears to have been
'renationalized'. One popular method for achieving a more
balanced appraisal of the arms trade at the national level involves
increasing parliamentary 'oversight' of the decision-making process;
standards would not only be applied at the correct level, but they
would also be seen to be applied. It is not that parliamentary
involvement would necessarily make any decision more moral,
rather that open discussion would enable moral arguments to be
heard and evaluated, itself an advancement ethically. With increased
parliamentary oversight, an individual exporter could in some way
help to limit the spread of weapons and technology simply by setting
an example of good behaviour. There would be scope for effective
inter-governmental co-operation of the sort achieved in the
Australia Group, CoCom and the Missile Technology Control
Regime, although it must be said that the effectiveness of these
initiatives depended to a large extent either on the discipline
engendered by the Cold War or on the existence of widely-held
WMD non-proliferation norms. Governments could seek further
harmonization of standards and practices, develop intelligence-
exchange mechanisms, and promote transparency initiatives such as

the UN Register of Conventional Arms – possibly the only international initiative which does not fall foul of the 'Article 51' argument. The aim could be to 'export' confidence as well as arms. But it is far from clear that any of this high-minded self-denial will be possible without further reducing, somehow, defence manufacturing capacity and making it possible for defence industries to survive without relying so heavily on exports

There is, finally, a fourth option. Supply-side governments, still unwilling or unable completely to discard traditional ideas of technology denial for strategic purposes, could resign themselves to restricting world access to a set of key, 'war-winning' technologies and applications. These technologies could include space weapons, information technology, communications and counter-communications, molecular engineering, artificial intelligence, robotics, nanotechnology, 'smart' weapons and materials, and advanced 'stealth' technology. If the international arms and technology market proves to be as diffuse and uncontrollable as many commentators are already suggesting, this minimalist strategy might be the best to hope for. But it is a strategy sure to provoke a counterbalancing response; there would be no opportunity for relaxation or complacency among the suppliers, and any advantage would be temporary, rather than innate. It is already difficult enough to apply traditional thinking about the arms trade and its control to the new, more vigorous and diffuse circumstances of the post-Cold War world. But in the twenty-first century the applications for newly developed military-related technologies and the difficulty – if not impossibility – of controlling access to such technologies, are likely to go far beyond what has been experienced, and imagined, in the 1990s.

BIBLIOGRAPHY

ACDA (Arms Control and Disarmament Agency), *World Military Expenditures and Arms Transfers*, 1993-1994 (Washington, D.C.: USGPO, 1995).

F. Ajami, 'The Summoning', *Foreign Affairs* (72/4,1993).

American Bar Association, *Beyond CoCom - A Comparative Study of Export Controls* (Washington, D.C., 1994).

I. Anthony (ed.) [1991], *Arms Export Regulations* (Oxford University Press for SIPRI, 1991).

I. Anthony [1993], 'The 'third tier' countries: production of major weapons', in H. Wulf (ed.), *Arms Industry Limited* (Oxford University Press for SIPRI, 1993).

D. Ball, 'Arms and Affluence: Military Acquisitions in the Asia-Pacific Region', *International Security* (18/3, 1993/4).

P. Batchelor and S. Willett, 'To trade or not to trade? The costs and benefits of South Africa's arms trade', *Military Research Group Working Papers* (no. 9, 1995).

R.A. Bitzinger, 'The Globalization of the Arms Industry: The Next Proliferation Challenge', *International Security* (19/2, 1994).

L. Blom-Cooper, *Guns for Antigua* (London: Duckworth, 1990).

Board of Social Responsibility, *Responsibility in Arms Transfer Policy* (London: General Synod of the Church of England, 1994).

M. Brzoska and F.S. Pearson, *Arms and Warfare: De-escalation and Negotiation* (University of South Carolina Press, 1994).

B. Buzan, *An Introduction to Strategic Studies: Military Technology & International Relations* (London: Macmillan/IISS, 1987).

A. Cassese, *Human Rights in a Changing World* (Cambridge: Polity Press, 1994).

G. Chafetz, 'The end of the Cold War and the future of nuclear proliferation: an alternative to the neorealist perspective', *Security Studies* (Summer 1993).

M. Chalmers and O. Greene, *Taking Stock: The UN Register After Two Years* (Oxford:Westview Press,1995).

M Chew, 'Human rights in Singapore: perceptions and problems', *Asian Survey* (34/11, November 1994)

P. Cornish, *The Arms Trade and Europe* (London: Pinter/RIIA, 1995).

Deltac/Saferworld, *Proliferation and Export Controls: An Analysis of Sensitive Technologies and Countries of Concern* (Deltac, 1995).

J. Donnelly, *International Human Rights* (Oxford: Westview Press, 1993).

J. Frankel, *International Relations in a Changing World* (Oxford University Press, 1991).

T.W. Galdi, *Advanced Weapons Technology: Export Controls Before and After the Cold War* (CRS Report for Congress, 93-22 F, 6 January 1993).

C.S. Gray, 'Arms control does not control arms', *Orbis* (37/3, 1993).

R. Harkavy, *The Arms Trade and International Systems* (Cambridge, Mass.: Ballinger, 1975).

G. Hartcup, *The Silent Revolution: Development of Conventional Weapons, 1945–85* (London: Brassey's, 1993).

G Hoffman, 'The Politics and Ethics of Military Intervention', *Survival* (37/4, 1995–96)

C. Hofhansel, 'From containment of communism to Saddam: the evolution of export control regimes', *Arms Control* (14/3, 1993).

House of Commons, Foreign Affairs Committee, *UK Policy on Weapons Proliferation and Arms Control in the Post-Cold War Era. Volume II: Minutes of Evidence and Appendices* (London: HMSO, 1995; FCO memorandum dated 6 July 1994).

S.P. Huntington [A], The clash of civilizations?, *Foreign Affairs* (72/3, 1993).

S.P. Huntington [B], 'If not civilizations, what? Paradigms of the Post–Cold War World', *Foreign Affairs* (72/5, 1993)

INSS (Institute for National Strategic Studies), *Strategic Assessment 1995: U.S. Security Challenges in Transition* (Washington, 1995).

J.J. Johnson, 'Conventional Arms Transfer Policy: An Industry Perspective', *Military Technology* (18/2, 1994).

A. Karp, 'The Demise of the Middle-East Arms Race', *The Washington Quarterly* (18/4, 1995).

J. Keegan, *A History of Warfare* (London: Hutchinson, 1993).

B. Kellman, 'Bridling the International Trade of Catastrophic Weaponry', *The American University Law Review* (43/3, 1994).

K. Krause, *Arms and the State: Patterns of Military Production and Trade* (Cambridge University Press, 1992).

J. M. Lamb and J. L. Moher, *Conventional Arms Transfers: Approaches to Multilateral Control in the 1990s* (Ottawa: CCACD, Aurora Papers, no. 13, 1992).

D.S. Landes, *The Unbound Prometheus: Technological Change and Industrial Development in Western Europe from 1750 to the Present* (Cambridge University Press, 1969).

E.J. Laurance [1992], *The International Arms Trade* (New York: Lexington, 1992).

E. J. Laurance [1993], 'Reducing the negative consequences of arms transfers through unilateral arms control', in B. Ramberg (ed.), *Arms Control Without Negotiation* (London: Lynne Rienner, 1993).

E. J. Laurance, S. T. Wezeman and H. Wulf, *Arms Watch: SIPRI Report on the First Year of the UN Register of Conventional Arms* (Oxford University Press for SIPRI, 1993).

K Mahbubani, 'The Dangers of Decadence: What the Rest Can Teach the West', *Foreign Affairs* (72/4, 1993).

C. Masefield, 'Defence exports: the challenge ahead', *Journal of the Royal United Services Institute* (140/4, 1995).

N.A.L. Mohammed, 'The development trap: militarism, environmental degradation and poverty in the South', in G. Tansey, F. Tansey and P. Rogers (eds.), *A World Divided: Militarism and Development after the Cold War* (London: Earthscan, 1994).

M. Moodie, 'Managing technology diffusion and non-proliferation in the post-Cold War era', *International Security Digest* (2/1, 1994).

H. Mueller, 'The Export Controls Debate in the 'New' European Community', *Arms Control Today* (23/2, 1993).

D. Mussington, *Understanding Contemporary International Arms Transfers* (London: IISS, 1994).

S.G. Neuman, 'Controlling the arms trade: idealistic dream or realpolitik?', *Washington Quarterly* (16/3, 1993).

T. Ohlson (ed.), *Arms Transfer Limitations and Third World Security* (Oxford University Press for SIPRI, 1988).

F.S. Pearson, *The Global Spread of Arms: Political Economy of International Security* (Oxford: Westview Press, 1994).

A.J. Pierre, *The Global Politics of Arms Sales* (Princeton University Press, 1982).

Pontifical Council for Justice and Peace, *The International Arms Trade: An Ethical Reflection* (Vatican City, 1994).

W.H. Reinicke, 'No stopping now: high-tech trade in the new global environment', *Brookings Review* (Spring 1994).

B. Roberts, 'From non-proliferation to anti-proliferation', *International Security* (18/1, 1993).

J. Sachs, *Faith in the Future* (London: Darton, Longman and Todd, 1995).

M. Sandström and C. Wilén, *A Changing European Defence Industry: The Trend Towards Internationalization in the Defence Industry of Western Europe* (Stockholm: Swedish Defence Research Establishment, 1993).

D. Shukman, *The Sorcerer's Challenge: Fears and Hopes for the Weapons of the Next Millennium* (London: Hodder & Stoughton, 1995).

J. Simpson, 'The nuclear non-proliferation regime as a model for conventional armament restraint', in Ohlson (ed.), *Arms Transfer Limitations.*

SIPRI [Stockholm International Peace Research Institute], *The Arms Trade with the Third World* (London: Paul Elek, 1971).

SIPRI, *World Armaments and Disarmament Yearbook 1993* (Oxford University Press for SIPRI, 1993).

J.G. Stoessinger, *Why Nations Go to War* (New York: St. Martin's Press, 1993).

T. Taylor, 'Conventional arms: the drives to export', in T. Taylor and R. Imai (eds.), *The Defence Trade: Demand, Supply and Control* (London: RIIA/IIPS, 1994).

A. and H. Toffler, *War and Anti-War: Making Sense of Today's Global Chaos* (London: Warner Books, 1995).

A.Toynbee, *The World and the West)* (Oxford: Oxford University Press , 1953).

UN (United Nations), *Study on Ways and Means of Promoting Transparency in International Transfers of Conventional Arms* (A/46/30, UNODA Study Series no.24, 1992).

P. van Ham, *Managing Non-Proliferation Regimes in the 1990s* (London: Pinter/RIIA, 1993).

M.B. Wallerstein and W.W. Snyder, 'The evolution of U.S. export control policy: 1949–1989', in *National Academy of Sciences, Finding Common Ground: U.S. Export Controls in a Changed Global Environment* (Washington, D.C.: National Academy Press, 1991).

S. Willett, 'Dragon's fire and tiger's claws: arms trade and production in Far East Asia', *Contemporary Security Policy* (15/2, 1994).

R. Williamson, *Profit without honour? Ethics and the Arms Trade* (London: CCADD, 1992).

H. Wulf (Ed.), *Arms Industry Limited* (Oxford University Press/SIPRI, 1993).

P.D. Zimmerman, 'Proliferation: bronze medal technology is enough', *Orbis* (38/1, 1994).

INDEX

absolutism, 97
Afghanistan, 50
Al Yamamah arms deal between the UK
and Saudi Arabia, 27
anti-personnel landmines, 49, 50, 53
Aristotle, 90
Armament Year-Book, 22
arms exports and foreign policy, 18–19
arms and technology transfers, 103
arms buyers, 27–29
arms export controls, 19, 46
arms markets, 26, 27, 41–4
arms race,17, 28–9
arms sales and transfers, secrecy of, 11
arms suppliers, 29–30
arms supply and demand, 31–2
arms trade: embargoes and restrictions,
47, 99; increased parliamentary oversight
at national level, 114; *laisser-faire*
approach to, 46; regulation of, 47;
arms transfer agreements and controls,
23, 105
Arnold Toynbee, 92
Asia–Pacific region, 5, 34, 95, 99, 105,
Australia, 68; Australia Group, 114
Austria, 55, 71

Baghdad, Iraq, 1991 bombardment of,
37
Bangkok, 99
BBC Reith Lectures, 1952, 92
biological weapons, 1, 61; see also
weapons of mass destruction
Bosnia, 100
Brazil, 30
bronze medal technologies, 40
Bulgaria, 30
Burma, see Myanmur

Cambodia, 50
Chechen rebels, 88
Chemical Weapons Convention, 62
chemical weapons, 1, 61; see also

weapons of mass destruction
China, 28, 30, 64, 70, 101, 103, 105
Churchill, Winston, 52
civilian and military technological
civilianization of technological
innovation, 32, 37–41, 109
Clausewitz, Karl von, 93
co-operative export control, 59–62
Committee for Multilateral Export
Controls (CoCom), 61, 64, 67–73, 114;
CoCom Co-operation Forum (CCF), 69
coercive trade-management regime, 61
Cold War, 1– 6, 11, 30, 31, 33, 46, 54,
56, 58, 59, 62, 63, 67, 69, 81, 83, 85, 86,
89, 90, 93, 94, 96, 107, 114
Communism, 100
communist insurgency campaigns, 29
competitive tendering for the supply of
arms and military equipment, 35
Conference on Security and Co-
operation in Europe (CSCE), 6, 64, 98,
98
Congressional Research Service (CRS),
23, 25
consolidation and restructuring in the
Conventional Armed Forces in Europe
(CFE), 21, 72, 85
conventional arms and related
technology, 1, 5, 9, 99, 105, 107
Coordination Committee for Multilateral
Export Controls, 7
Council of the League of Nations,
periodical statistics on the international
arms trade, 22
covert arms trade, 44
Czech Republic, 71

Declaration on Conventional Arms
Transfers and NBC Non-Proliferation,
63
defence contracts, 32
defence conversion, 2
defence industry, internationalization and

diffusion of, 16–18, 33, 35, 37, 107
defence-related infrastructure and trade, 23, 60, 61, 53, 59
democracy, 99, 104; and democratic freedoms, 112; and democratic values, 101
Deng Xiaoping, 101
direct technology transfers, 35
diversification, 2
domestic defence, 81–2
dual-use technology, 6, 15, 23, 38, 57, 72, 102

East–West relations, 1, 5, 54, 107
Economist, The 100
Egypt, 30
embargoes and economic sanctions, 60, 91, 105
European Commission, 55, 76
European Community, 6, 64, 76
European Union Initiatives, 73
European Union's eight criteria, 98
European Union, 68, 103; arms criteria, 75; 'dual-use' technology export control regulation, 7, 77–9
Exclusive Economic Zones, 29
export control systems, 15, 34, 38, 41, 42, 54, 61, 78

Far East, 29
Financial Times, 100
Finland, 71
World War I, 51
fishing rights, protecting, 29
foreign policy, 107; and arms exports, 18–19
Fort Worth, Texas, 36
France, 25, 29, 54, 60, 70, 73
free trade, 103

Germany, 29, 55, 73, 103
Global Positioning Satellite, 39
global telecommunications revolution, 80
Golan Heights, 87
Great Britain, see United Kingdom

Group of Governmental Experts, 67
Group of Seven leading industrialized democracies (G7), 63; and 'Declaration on Conventional Arms Transfers and NBC Non-Proliferation', 6, 98
'Guidelines for Conventional Arms Transfers', 64
Gulf War, 27, 37, 56, 57, 63–5, 73

Hague, The, 71
Henderson, Paul, 57
historical and cultural relativism, 90
History of Warfare (John Keegan), 93
House of Commons, 6, 18, 55, 83
human rights, 60, 64, 99, 101, 103, 104, 112
Hungary, 70, 71

Iceland, 68
illegal arms market, size of, 43
import of arms and military equipment, 12–15
India, 30
India, partition of in 1947, 50
individual freedoms, 99, 104
Indonesia, 34
information technology, 115
Institute for National Security Studies (INSS), 92, 93
Intergovernmental Conference on Political Union, 74
International Atomic Energy List (IAEL), 68
International Committee of the Red Cross, 98
International Herald Tribune, 100
International Industrial List (IIL), 68
International Munitions List (IML), 68
international arms market, 10, 11, 20–37, 47, 61, 78, 80, 82, 89, 91, 104, 107, 108, 111, 112, 113, 115
international law, 48–49, 84, 103, 104
Iran, 27, 36, 56, 70, 72
Iraq, 6, 13, 36, 56,63, 72, 74, 81
Ireland, 71
Israel, 30, 42, 74, 87